SATIRE, COMEDY AND MENTAL HEALTH

SATIRE, COMEDY AND MENTAL HEALTH

Coping with the Limits of Critique

DIETER DECLERCQ
University of Kent, UK

emerald
PUBLISHING

United Kingdom – North America – Japan – India
Malaysia – China

Emerald Publishing Limited
Howard House, Wagon Lane, Bingley BD16 1WA, UK

First edition 2021

British Library Cataloguing in Publication Data
A catalogue record for this book is available from the British Library

ISBN: 978-1-83909-667-9 (Print)
ISBN: 978-1-83909-666-2 (Online)
ISBN: 978-1-83909-668-6 (Epub)

Printed and bound by CPI Group (UK) Ltd, Croydon, CR0 4YY

ISOQAR certified Management System, awarded to Emerald for adherence to Environmental standard ISO 14001:2004.

ISOQAR REGISTERED
Certificate Number 1985
ISO 14001

INVESTOR IN PEOPLE

For my parents and Georgia.

CONTENTS

ABOUT THE AUTHOR

Dr Dieter Declercq is a Lecturer in Film and Media Studies at the University of Kent. He is interested in the existential value of popular media (especially satire, comedy and cartoons) and his research is informed by methodologies from analytic aesthetics, media studies, and medical and health humanities. He has organised several international events, including the British Society of Aesthetics Conference: Art, Aesthetics and the Medical and Health Humanities. His work on satire, comedy and irony has been published in journals including *The Journal of Aesthetics and Art Criticism*, *ImageText*, *Ethical Perspectives* and *Ethical Theory and Moral Practice*.

ACKNOWLEDGEMENTS

I remember when I first started thinking about satire in an academic context. It was 2009 and I had no idea what to write about for my MA dissertation in Western Literature. Then, something or someone made me realise that I could pretty much write my dissertation about anything. Really? Anything? Even *The Simpsons*? Although I wrote that first dissertation on Shakespeare adaptations, my real interest was always more existential than literary. *The Simpsons* had been a beacon that shone through as I experienced a spell of alienation in high school (who didn't?). Still, however strong the estrangement, *The Simpsons* was just so funny and, well, so right about things, that it always gave me an entry point for reconnection with the world (albeit with a sense of comic irony). This book is, therefore, grounded in my personal relationship with the solace of satire.

Many people have contributed to the development of my ideas in this book along the way – too many to list them all from the beginning. I do want to foremost acknowledge my parents and my fiancée Georgia, to whom I dedicate this book. Without my parents, I would not have written this book (and I do not mean that in the biological sense of things). I am privileged that they have always supported my studies, including at times when I was unsure that it was really going somewhere. I am also indebted to Georgia, for giving me the space to pursue my academic projects, and for her support during those moments when I am still not sure whether it's going anywhere. She's also been an invaluable soundboard for the ideas in this book. I also want to thank Ben Doyle, for signing me with Emerald, and the great editorial team at Emerald, Paula Kennedy, Joshi Jerome, Sally Martin, Liam Morris, Gabriella Barnard-Edmunds and Carys Morley. Thanks also to S. Rajachitra for help during the production process.

This book is a substantially revised and updated version of a PhD thesis which I completed at the University of Kent in 2017, where I still teach and work. I'm very grateful for the School of Arts' support of that project with a 50th Anniversary GTA Scholarship. I'm also indebted to my supervisor, Aylish Wood, for her invaluable (and continued) guidance and support in my academic career. I also want to thank my co-supervisor (and compatriot), Hans

Maes, for introducing me to analytic aesthetics and philosophy of art. Life is a funny (and sometimes scary) accumulation of contingencies, but without the fantastic Aesthetic Research Centre, my professional and personal life would have been much impoverished. Thanks also to fellow ARC members, Michael Newall, for his openness to explore commonalities with the medical and health humanities, and (my internal examiner) Murray Smith, for guidance and inspiration. I also want to thank my external examiner, Gregory Currie, for his academic rigour.

There are many others to thank in the vibrant research culture of the School of Arts. I specifically acknowledge my fellow PhD students at the time, with whom I exchanged ideas on a regular basis in Work in Progress Sessions and the Postgraduate Hub, including Eleen Deprez, Claire Anscombe, Mark Windsor, Shelby Moser, Sara Janssen and especially David Brown (for fruitful debate about shared research interests). Thanks also to Fred Francis and Julia Secklehner for co-curating an exhibition with many cartoons that informed discussions in this book. I also want to thank my colleagues, Nicola Shaughnessy, for support and collaboration around medical and health humanities, and Oliver Double, for support and collaboration around comedy. My thanks also to many people who have commented on various aspects of this research project at conferences and other events, and to the British Society of Aesthetics for several travel stipends which allowed me to disseminate my ideas.

Some of the ideas in this book are based on previously published work. Chapter 1 revisits key ideas (and sometimes examples) from my 2018 article 'A Definition of Satire (And Why a Definition Matters)' in *Journal of Aesthetics and Art Criticism, 76*(3), 319–330. Chapters 3 and 5 elaborate on ideas about moral imperfection and ironic characters developed in my 2020 article 'Irony, Disruption and Moral Imperfection' in *Ethical Theory and Moral Practice,* 23(3), 545–559.

ABSTRACT

Satire, Comedy and Mental Health: Coping with the Limits of Critique examines how satire helps to sustain good mental health in a troubled socio-political world. Through an interdisciplinary dialogue, which combines approaches from analytic philosophy of art, medical and health humanities, media studies and psychology, Dr Dieter Declercq (University of Kent) frames satire as a resource for coping with a sick world beyond full recovery.

Satire has the purpose to critique and entertain – which explains the genre's infamous ambiguity. Critique is a moral activity which opposes social wrongness, while entertainment involves leisurely enjoying aesthetic pleasures. Satire is, therefore, not the most efficient or impactful means of critique. Yet, instead of curing a sick world, satire helps us cope with it.

Although satire can contribute to social change by motivating activism, satirists also acknowledge that political action is not always successful and that our own resources for critique are not endless. These limits of critique introduce mental health challenges, like depression and neurotic perfectionism, as we must deal with suffering that we cannot alleviate (and to which we may even be complicit).

Satire contributes to coping because its ambiguous combination of critique and entertainment negotiates a balance between care for others and care of self. This book investigates how we can adopt and adapt aesthetic strategies from satire, especially comic irony, to cope with the limits of critique – through philosophical explication and close analysis of satire in various media (including novels, music, TV, film, cartoons, memes, stand-up comedy and protest artefacts).

INTRODUCTION

AIMS

What is satire, what can it do or not do and why should we care about it? Since the Romans coined 'satire' as a classification of art, these questions have been continually addressed by satirists themselves, their fans, detractors, political and moral authorities, art critics and, last but not least, scholars from a variety of disciplines. The result is a myriad of longstanding discussions about satire which have often been fruitful and enlightening. Still, the fundamental questions about satire's nature, function and significance remain a matter of debate.

The reception of satire has been ambiguous. Scholars and critics have hailed satire for its moral and political interventions (Jones, 2010) as well as its amoral aesthetic pleasures (Grigson, 1980) – while sceptics have condemned the genre as immoral cynicism (Hart, 2013). There is no consensus whether satire is a punitive but curative practice (Tucholsky, 1919) that is deadly for political opponents (Jones, 2014); whether its political impact is only more moderately incremental (Day, 2011) or even ethereal (Quirk, 2015); or whether satire is really like a safety valve (Gini, 2017) that facilitates political acquiescence (Nokes, 1987) by venting anger and frustration (Njoya 2017).

What has often remained unacknowledged in these debates is that satire's ambiguous reception itself signals a central ambiguity in the genre. Satire has both the moral purpose to critique social wrongness and the aesthetic purpose to entertain. Most approaches to satire have typically subordinated one of the genre's central purposes to the other. Some scholars have argued that entertainment in satire really supports its political aims (McClennen, 2011), while others have downplayed the genre's moral purpose to promote its aesthetic pleasures (Griffin, 1994), decry its cynicism (Webber, 2013) or frame satire as an emotional catharsis (Freedman, 2008).

I argue that satire's moral and aesthetic purposes are equally important and that we should frame the genre's purposeful ambiguity in relation to mental health. This position differs significantly from the idea that satire is a safety valve that provides an emotional catharsis by venting negative emotions like anger and frustration, which could otherwise be put to political action. For one, such a hydraulic understanding of the emotions is outdated (Evans, 2003), while the safety valve metaphor is opaque and does not actually clarify how satire works. Moreover, the catharsis model cannot accommodate that satire is also genuinely committed to critique and can have (modest) political impact. Yet, satire is significant because it also alleviates the limits of critique and political action – which is why the solace of entertainment matters.

Satire's ambiguous interaction between critique and entertainment resonates with an existential conflict between the care for others and care of self. We have a moral duty to care for others and alleviate their suffering, which is the domain of critique. However, if we tried to devote ourselves unabatedly to critique, we would compromise our own wellbeing. For one, our resources to sustain critique and political action are limited – and if we tried to devote ourselves unabatedly to critique, we would set ourselves unattainable goals and fall prey to the mental suffering of neurotic perfectionism (Geranmayepoura & Besharata, 2010). Moreover, the political impact of critique is also limited; sometimes, all the political action in the world is not enough to resolve a conflict and alleviate suffering.

The painful upshot of this situation is what I call 'the limits of critique', which means we must live in a world where suffering exists that we cannot alleviate and to which we may even be complicit. We may experience such a world as patently absurd, and become disconnected from it, which introduces the risk of depression (Godderis, 2000). Just consider mental health conditions like political depression (Cvetkovich, 2012) or eco-anxiety (Stoknes, 2015), which occur when people face problems which seem too overwhelming to resolve. The main argument of this book is that good satire helps us cope with the limits of critique by avoiding the Scylla of political apathy and the Charybdis of mental health problems. Therefore, satire is a resource to negotiate the existential conflict between care for others and care of self.

The main aim of *Satire, Comedy and Mental Health* is to investigate how we can use satire as a resource in our own lives to deal with the limits of critique. The book develops three key arguments. First, satire does not really cure a morally sick world, but helps us to cope with it. This does not mean that satire cannot contribute to political change, but it only has a modest impact in the service of motivating more direct political action. Second, satire helps us deal with the limits of critique through the solace of pleasurable autotelic engrossment in entertainment, which reconnects us to an otherwise depressingly absurd world – without ignoring that we should alleviate suffering where we can. Third, satire develops comic and ironic coping strategies that we can fruitfully adopt and adapt in the stories we tell about ourselves in a world that is sick beyond full recovery.

METHOD

In this study, I approach satires as intentionally designed artefacts with specific affordances (or useful aspects) – which is a common methodology in analytic philosophy of art (see Currie, 2010; Maynard, 2012). Satires are artefacts that are designed for a certain purpose, namely to critique and entertain. Due to this intentionally designed purpose, satires have specific affordances, including motivating or sustaining political action and, most importantly, coping with the limits of critique. We can establish these affordances through analysis of satire's intentional design.

This methodology approaches satire as a tool, like a hammer. One of the key affordances of hammers is to drive nails into walls, which we know by analysing their intentional design. Hammers typically have long handles (in wood or plastic) and a weighted metal head. They are intentionally designed so that the long handle affords a good grip to swing the head onto the surface of a nail with appropriate force to drive it into a wall. By contrast, you cannot eat soup with a hammer (you really need a spoon) – which, again, we know through artefactual analysis. Yet, although most hammers are also not designed to open beer bottles, they do afford this use – but still only by virtue of their artefactual design.

Similarly, I approach satires as narrative artefacts that are designed to tell stories that critique and entertain. Satires are often professionally produced narratives like cartoons, novels or films; but we can equally tell a satirical joke or make a satirical remark. These jokes and remarks are typically (part of) a story – often just a 'mini-narrative' – about what someone did or should have done (Williams, 2002, p. 233). We need not publicly express or share these satirical narratives with others; we can also simply think through sequences of thought, feeling and imagination with a narrative structure (Goldie, 2012, pp. 4–5). As narrative artefacts, satires are resources that help us make sense of ourselves and the challenges to our mental health in a world that is sick beyond full recovery (see also Guerrero, 2019).

Narratives are artefacts that are intentionally designed to communicate meaning through stories (Currie, 2010, p. 6). Hence, narrative interpretation is guided by communicative principles (Currie, 2004, p, 112). According to the relevance theory, we decode the meaning of a communicative utterance by inferring the most optimally relevant interpretation of a thought which it resembles in content (Sperber & Wilson, 2012, p. 127). If I tell my dinner companions, 'Can you pass me the salt?', the most relevant interpretation is to interpret that utterance as evidence that I wish to put salt on my food (not pepper) – unless I am making a snarky ironic comment about the sodium levels in the fast food we ordered. Similarly, according to Gregory Currie's (2004) theory of narrative interpretation, 'we use the text, together with various other things, to come up with the best ideas we can about what the author intended to convey' (p. 109).

Crucially, Currie (2004) does not advocate that we seek to establish authorial intentions irrespective of textual evidence (p. 125). For example, suppose that we unearth a long-lost diary of Jonathan Swift in which he asserts that *A Modest Proposal* was really intended to outline a new and revolutionary model for calculus. This discovery does not mean that we should change our interpretation of Swift's famous satire. As Currie (2004) explains, it is what Swift has written in his text that constrains narrative interpretation 'in ways that no other source of evidence does' (p. 126). In other words, Swift's assertions about the meaning of *A Modest Proposal* are irrelevant if they cannot be reasonably inferred from the text.

Nonetheless, satirists are skilled and reflexive artists who know what they are doing – often better than anybody else. Hence, throughout this book, I engage with various comments that satirists themselves have made about their satire – including Samantha Bee, Matt Bors, Stephen Colbert, Aaron McGruder, John Oliver, Dan Perkins (aka Tom Tomorrow), Jen Sorensen, Jon Stewart and Ted Rall. In various ways, these satirists have argued that satire is a resource to sustain good mental health in a troubled socio-political world.

Yet, I only draw on these comments to substantiate arguments about satire's coping affordances as long as they can be inferred from close analysis of a wide range of works in diverse media – including novels (Margaret Atwood's *The Handmaid's Tale*), music (Jimi Hendrix's 'Star-Spangled Banner'), stand-up comedy (Stewart Lee), TV (*South Park*'s 'The Hobbit'), film (Stanley Kubrick's *Dr Strangelove*), cartoons (Aaron McGruder's *The Boondocks*), memes (Trump piñatas) and protest artefacts (Tump Baby blimp).

These close analyses, supported by relevant comments of satirists, will ground my argument about the coping affordances of satire. I argue that satires are artefacts designed to critique and entertain, with purposeful affordances to cope with the limits of critique. Satire's artefactual design reveals that instead of devoting all available resources to critique, satirists also entertain – which (only) makes sense if we know that critique has its limits and entertainment involves autotelic engrossment in aesthetic pleasures which allows us to cope with those limits. These entertaining strategies, especially comic irony, not only distance us from the limits of critique, but also reframe the meaning of these limits from a less threatening perspective.

Many comments by satirists reveal that creating satire is perhaps foremost a therapy for themselves (although, of course, it also helps to pay the bills). Still, satirists typically also create satire in the hope that it has coping affordances for their audiences (even if that is far less under their control). Satire is obviously designed for media consumption and I will draw on research in psychology – especially the Revised Transactional Model of Coping (Folkman, 2008) and the Mood Management Theory (Robinson & Knobloch-Westerwick, 2016) – to substantiate the hypothesis that consuming entertainment in the right measure has valuable affordances to sustain good mental health.

Yet, my investigation also moves beyond media consumption to outline the coping affordances of satire to ordinary media users, especially satirical strategies of comic irony. I will establish the coping affordances of comic irony in dialogue with scholarship from the psychology of humour (Kuiper, 2012; Martin, 2006) and I will argue that we can adopt and adapt satirical strategies, like comic irony, in the stories we tell about ourselves in a troubled world, drawing on narrative frameworks from philosophy (Goldie, 2010; Lindemann, 2001) and the medical and health humanities (Charon, 2006; Frank, 1995). Although I doubt that satirists design their satire with such narrative appropriation in mind, it is still an affordance of satire by virtue of the genre's artefactual design – just like hammers are designed to drive nails into walls but also afford to open beer bottles.

My arguments about the artefactual design of satire are subject to empirical verification and falsification. Through narrative interpretation, I will make claims about the meaning and affordances of satire which are accurate or not (so, hopefully, I will not be making claims similar to the assertion that *A Modest Proposal* outlines a model for calculus). Put metaphorically, suppose I was to embark on a study about hammers, I would be making claims that we can verify by looking at them and investigating their design; and refute by claiming that I have mistaken what hammers actually look like or that my selected sample is too narrow or otherwise not representative of hammers in general.

Nevertheless, in my hypothetical hammer study, I would make claims about their afforded uses without empirically establishing what people really do with hammers or measuring how effective they are at driving nails into the wall. In other words, my actual study of satire will introduce arguments about the coping affordances of the genre without providing evidence of what people do with satire or how effective it is as a coping strategy. Although I will develop my arguments in dialogue with relevant empirical evidence from the natural and social sciences (especially psychology), my own methodology is humanistic, which introduces unavoidable, but purposeful, limitations to my study.

Currently, a meaningful empirical study of how satire contributes to coping with the limits of critique feels somewhat like a pipe dream – exactly because a book like *Satire, Comedy and Mental Health* needs to be written first to establish if and how satire is artefactually designed for coping. Without such a foundational study, meaningful empirical research is currently hard to conceive. In this respect, there is a large body of sound research in communication studies about satire's political impact on audiences which has been largely inconclusive (see Holbert, 2013; Young, 2018). The problem with this kind of empirical research about satire is not the soundness of the methodologies, but the lack of clarity about what exactly they should set out to measure.

The ambiguous reception in scholarship and criticism indicates that it is unclear what satire is *designed* to achieve – let alone what individual satires *actually* achieve. Without greater certainty about the artefactual design of satire, empirical studies may well investigate unhelpful directions. Imagine that hammers were more complex artefacts (a bit like satires); as long as we have not investigated what they are designed for, we risk wasting our time with studies that try to establish how people use hammers for eating soup. Presently, there are two common misconceptions about satire which risk causing confusion about future directions for empirical research. The first misconception is that the significance of the genre should be narrowly framed in terms of political impact. The second is that, conversely, satire offers an emotional catharsis that helps us cope with a troubled socio-political world – but at the expense of dissipating all motivation for political action.

Satire, Comedy and Mental Health aims to redress this situation by developing a theoretical model for understanding satire's coping affordances, which does not deny the genre's modest political affordances, and is also informed by scholarship about coping and mental health. At this stage, I consider a philosophical study of satire's artefactual design more appropriate than trying to document how audiences use satire for coping (through interviews or focus groups). Although people may be able to explain *what* they do with satire or *how* it makes them feel, they do not necessarily know *why* it has those affordances. Similarly, although I could tell you that my word processor afforded me to write this book, I could not explain the underlying process behind this affordance.

Moreover, I imagine that there will always be significant challenges for empirical research into the coping effects of satire. Satire is not some tonic or medicine. We should not think of satire as something to consume twice a day (once in the morning and once in the evening), if we feel mild to moderate existential despair about suffering that we cannot alleviate (and to which we may even be complicit). Moreover, we should equally not think of satire as the only coping strategy in this situation – at the expense other strategies like physical activity or psychotherapy. Therefore, it may prove difficult to set up an experiment to measure the coping effects of satire that controls for all the variables.

Instead, we should think of satire as a tool we can use if we experience feelings of existential despair about the limits of critique. In general, the efficiency of tools depends on multiple variables, including the aptitude and skill of the user, alongside their state of mind or even level of intoxication. Put differently, some people are more naturally skilled with hammers, although they do become harder to handle for almost anybody after having opened too many beer bottles and drinking their contents. Yet, what we can say with certainty is that, for everyone in all circumstances, it is much more difficult to try and drive a nail into a wall without a hammer.

Similarly, *Satire, Comedy and Mental Health* aims to unpack why we would lose an invaluable tool for coping with the limits of critique if we ignored satire in our existential toolbox. I do hope that a future and more ambitious project than mine can establish satire's contributions to coping with more empirical certainty – which I think would have to be a project that combines expertise from across the humanities, social sciences and natural sciences. I also hope that my book can help to pave the way for such a future study.

CHAPTER OUTLINE

The rest of this book has five more chapters. The first chapter argues that satire is a genre with the moral purpose to critique and the aesthetic purpose to entertain. Although these moral and aesthetic purposes of satire fruitfully interact, they also pull in different directions, which makes satire at once distinct, ambiguous and relevant to the study of mental health.

The second chapter challenges the heroic conception of satire as a therapy for the socio-political ills of the world. I do not deny that satire has political affordances, but these should be primarily conceptualised as harnessing emotional resources to stimulate or sustain other forms of political action, which have greater political impact. As (what I call) a 'magic' representation, satire can serve as an emotional booster to stimulate or sustain political action. However, such political action does not always entail political success. The idea of satire as a heroic therapy that cures socio-political sickness, therefore, introduces expectations that the genre cannot meet. Moreover, since the political impact of satire is only modest, especially compared to direct forms of political action, narrowly framing the genre's significance in terms of its political impact may ultimately make satire seem less significant than it really is.

The third chapter instead frames satire as a therapy for a world which is sick beyond full recovery. I argue that reflexive satirists are aware of the 'limits of critique' which confront us with suffering that we cannot alleviate, and to which we may even be complicit. The limits of critique highlight an existential tension between the care for others and care of self, which introduces mental health challenges like neurotic perfectionism and depression. Satire seeks to alleviate these mental health challenges, but to understand why and how, we need to move beyond the catharsis model.

The fourth chapter argues that satire contributes to emotion-focussed coping with the limits of critique by providing pleasurable aesthetic engrossment that lifts our mood and helps to sustain meaning in an absurd world. Satire's significance is that its central tension between critique and entertainment serves as a coping resource to negotiate the existential conflict between care for others and care of self.

The fifth chapter turns to comic irony as a satirical strategy for meaning-focussed coping which actively reframes how we think about the limits of critique. I argue that satire introduces comic and ironic strategies – like analogy, reversal and (what I call) 'ironic characters' – which we can integrate in the stories we develop about our moral imperfection in a morally imperfect world.

1

WHAT IS SATIRE?

INTRODUCTION

In this chapter, I investigate what satire is, what makes it so distinct and why it is relevant to the study of mental health. Satire is a genre with the purpose to critique and entertain. This means that identifying some creative expression as satire introduces the expectation that it both critiques social wrongness and provides entertaining aesthetic pleasures. Although these moral and aesthetic functions of satire fruitfully interact, they also pull in different directions. Critique introduces the demands of moral commitment, while entertainment distracts from the serious business of life. This central combination of critique and entertainment generates a fundamental ambiguity in satire, which makes the genre relevant to the study of mental health.

VARIETY

Satire has been around for a long time, across a variety of cultures. The origins of the word 'satire' are Latin and associated with meanings of 'fullness' and 'variety' (Gowers, 2012). In the third century BCE, the Roman poet Ennius first introduced *Saturae* as the title for a varied medley of poems (Braund, 1996, p. xi). A century later, Lucilius adopted the label for his sardonic and morally critical poetry (Freudenburg, 2001, p. 25). Lucilius's model again inspired later generations of satirists, including Horace and Juvenal, who became perhaps the most enduring prototypes of the genre (Jones, 2007, p. ix-1; McClennen, 2016).

However, the Romans may have introduced the label 'satire', but they did not invent the artistic practice. For one, although the ancient Greeks did not have a word equivalent to satire, Roman satirists like Horace acknowledged the influence of Aristophanes and other comic playwrights, who ridiculed politicians and powerful social figures (Witke, 1970, p. 21). Moreover, satirical poems and songs about Chinese emperors in China date back to at least the first and the second century BCE (Knechtges, 1971, pp. 91–94).

Satire is an artistic practice that has grown organically across different cultures. For example, the poets of pre-Islamic tribes created *hija*, a form of aggressive ridicule directed towards enemies which is commonly considered as equivalent to satire (Elliott, 1960, pp. 15–18). Similarly, the indigenous Khoikhoi people in South Africa developed satirical stories in their orature at the time of Dutch colonisation (Wittenberg, 2014). Such historical and geographical variety suggests that satire 'rests on a substratum of ritual and folk behaviour' (Test, 1991, p. 9).

Satire also exceeds artistic contexts, as we can engage in satirical practices in our everyday lives. Consider online protest against the visit of Chinese president Xi Jinping to the Philippines in November 2018. Many Philippine Twitter users changed their profile pictures to Winnie the Pooh and shared hybrid Winnie the Pooh/Xi Jinping memes or wished each other 'Happy National Winnie the Pooh Day' (Filipino Times Staff, 2018). They did so because various media had reported that the Chinese government censured online memes of Winnie the Pooh, because netizens were satirising a perceived likeness between the fictional bear and their president.

Likewise, consider British MEP Nigel Farage's infamous and satirical takedown of the first President of the European Council, Herman van Rompuy. Perhaps Britain's most prominent Eurosceptic, Farage (2010) quipped that the EU's foremost representative had 'the charisma of a damp rag, and the appearance of a low-grade bank clerk'. He further accused van Rompuy of ideological anti-nationalism, sneering 'perhaps that's because you come from Belgium, which of course is pretty much a non-country' (2010). Whatever one thinks of Farage's politics, his rhetoric in the European Parliament would not have been out of place on a late-night satire show.

GENRE

Satire's diffuse origins and its great variety have caused much scholarly disagreement about what 'it' is. Many have argued that satire is not a genre of art (like the sitcom or romcom), but instead a 'spirit' with manifestations 'almost as various as cultural activity itself' (Condren, Davis, McCausland, & Phiddian, 2008, p. 443; see also Elliott, 1960, p. viii; Sutherland, 1958, p. 1; Test, 1991, p. 10; Wight, 1964 [1936], p. 2; Witke, 1970, p. 21). Moreover, when it does apply to art, many have argued that the label 'satire' does not function as a genre, but as a mode (Condren, 2012, p. 394; Fowler, 1985, p. 110; Griffin, 1994, p. 4; Witke, 1970, p. 21).

The traditional difference between genres and modes is that the former are art-kinds with fixed forms and structures, while the latter consist of non-structural features which modify art-kinds (Fowler, 1985, p. 56). In other words, satire is a mode because it does not have a fixed form or structure but modifies other genres like the sitcom or cartoon. Indeed, works of satire are often hybrids, like Jordan Peele's *Get Out*, which is equally a satire (of contemporary race relations in the USA) and a horror film. Similarly, sometimes, only some parts of a work are satirical, including comedies. Consider *Broad City*, a comedy series about how two millennial friends fail at 'adulting' in New York, which also includes satirical moments that target the gig economy or the living conditions of tenants in NYC.

However, it does not follow that satire is, therefore, not a genre. I do not understand genre as an art-kind with a fixed form or structure. Instead, genres are historically developed frameworks to make sense of not just art and media, but also ordinary communication (Biber & Conrad, 2009 p. 79). For example, when a friend turns to you and says, 'Knock, knock', you need to frame that utterance in the genre of knock–knock jokes to make sense of it. The same goes for artistic genres, although they do not just help us make sense of artworks, but also to evaluate them (Abell, 2015). In other words, genre classification introduces expectations about what a work sets out to do and how successfully it does it.

Take the *Austin Powers* films, which feature the inept villain, Dr Evil. In *Austin Powers: International Man of Mystery* (dir. Roach, 1997), Dr Evil cryogenically freezes himself in 1967 and awakes 30 years later. He immediately sets out to steal a nuclear warhead and threatens to blow up the world, unless the United Nations pay him … 'One million dollars!' However, rather than fear, Dr Evil's request is met with ridicule since he forgot to account for 30 years' worth of inflation. He might as well have asked for free concert tickets to his favourite band.

Crucially, Dr Evil's representation as an inept villain only makes sense in the genre of the spy parody. Imagine a similar performance in a spy thriller. It would be near incomprehensible if James Bond faced a criminal kingpin who was a bumbling fool because there would be no real threat to overcome. An inept *Bond* villain would also be a real let-down because there would be no suspense. By contrast, since a spy parody like *Austin Powers* sets out to mock the conventions of the spy thriller, Mike Myers's performance as the inept Dr Evil is not only intelligible, but also successful.

Genres are conceptual frameworks that guide audience interpretation and evaluation. I propose that the label 'satire' similarly operates as a genre classification. In other words, identifying some form of expression as satire frames what that expression sets out to do and how well it does it. This role of the label 'satire' is particularly clear when it is applied to creative expression in contexts unfamiliar with that label – like the plays of ancient Greece or the orature of the Khoikhoi people.

If genres are conceptual frameworks, rather than art-kinds with fixed structures or forms, the common distinction between modes and genres is superfluous. The fact that there are often hybrids between satire and other genres, or that there are sometimes only *parts* of works which can be classified as satirical, does not prevent satire from being a genre. In those cases, the label 'satire' still frames our understanding and appreciation of those works, but only in part, and alongside other genre classifications. As a conceptual framework, the label 'satire' can also frame expectations about activities in non-artistic settings – similar to derivative genre classifications like 'epic' or 'tragic'.

A particularly fruitful understanding of genre is the idea that 'every genre has a characteristic purpose' (Abell, 2015, p. 31). Broadly speaking, the broad generic purpose of comedy is to amuse its audience. Therefore, a performance that is labelled 'comedy', but fails to amuse, will not get positive reviews. Of course, comedies can include aspects that are not designed to amuse. Hannah Gadsby's stand-up comedy show *Nanette* received much praise because of its many serious moments about mental ill health. Nonetheless, on the whole, comedies set out to amuse, because we will not classify a work with a different overall purpose as 'comedy'.

So, what is satire's generic purpose? There is a consensus that satire is too varied (or 'protean') to be defined (Hodgart, 1969, p. 13; Jones, 2007, p. 1; Kernan, 1959, p. 7; Test, 1991, p. 256). According to Conal Condren (2012), at best, we can outline a list of features shared by many satires, but none of those features are necessary or sufficient for satire. There is no such exhaustive list, but I imagine it would include features like absurdity, amusement, analogy, attack, exaggeration, fantasy, grotesquery, humour, irony, moral criticism, ridicule, transgression, etc.

However, such a long and inconclusive list of features overlooks that satire has a central generic purpose. I have previously coined a definition of satire as a genre with the purpose to critique and entertain – with the qualification that these purposes interact, although neither is wholly instrumental to the other (Declercq, 2018a). This definition also underpins my project here, although I do not seek to rigorously defend it. Instead, I settle for a moderate claim that an interaction between critique and entertainment is central to *most* satire, which is why the genre is a valuable resource to sustain good mental health. Hence, sceptics who deny that my definition adequately defines all satire need not automatically extend that scepticism to my argument about satire and mental health.

Identifying a central interaction between critique and entertainment in satire is more useful than a long and inconclusive list of shared features because it helps to frame the genre's ambiguous reception. Scholars and critics have identified satire as a moral cure for social illness (Tucholsky, 1919), an amoral aesthetic pursuit (Griffin, 1994) and an immoral dismissal of political action (Webber, 2013). This ambiguity follows from a fundamental doubleness in satire's generic purpose to critique and entertain.

Margaret Atwood (2012) has captured the ambiguity of satire's doubleness in the reception of her novel, *The Handmaid's Tale*. Atwood's satirical prediction about an ultra-conservative militia that takes control of the US government focusses on the plight of a specific social cast, the handmaids, who have been forced to serve as surrogate mothers for the political elite during a global fertility crisis. In the novel, the handmaids wear long red dresses, with white caps and heavy boots. What struck Atwood is the ambiguous appropriation of these outfits by fans of the novel. Atwood (2012) explains that

> *[r]evellers dress up as Handmaids on Hallowe'en and also for protest marches – these two uses of its costumes mirroring its doubleness. Is it entertainment or dire political prophecy? Can it be both?*

My answer to Atwood's question is, yes, because satire is a genre with the purpose to critique and entertain. In other words, when we classify a form of creative expression as satire, we frame it as setting out to critique some social wrongness as well as offering aesthetic pleasures associated with entertainment. These moral and aesthetic purposes interact in satire, although neither is wholly instrumental to the other – and they ultimately also pull in different directions, which makes the genre ambiguous. In the next chapters, I argue why this ambiguity between critique and entertainment makes satire a valuable resource to sustain good mental health in a troubled socio-political world. For now, I develop a deeper understanding of satire and its central purpose to critique and entertain.

CRITIQUE

Critique, as I understand it, is the committed moral opposition against a target, sustained by an analysis of that target's perceived social wrongness. The origins of this conception of critique are philosophical. Simon Critchley (2001) argues that philosophers need to scrutinise the soundness of social discourses and practices to advance wellbeing (pp. 72–73). Philosophical critique involves truth-speaking about a crisis in society which needs to be resolved to achieve emancipation from injustice (Williams, 2002, pp. 219–224). In Western philosophy, the original critical impulse starts with Socrates, who concerned himself for the wellbeing of his contemporaries by challenging them to emancipate themselves from conventional wisdom (Bronner, 2011, p. 1).

Comparisons between satire and philosophy are common in scholarship (see Declercq, 2013). Satirists are commonly compared to Socrates, the 'horse-fly' who aimed to emancipate society by stinging his fellow citizens out of complacency (Branham Bracht, 2009, p. 148) – often using humour and irony in the process (Test, 1991, p. 23). For example, Jeffrey Jones (2010, p. 85) refers to Bill Maher as a 'presidential gadfly'. Another ancient philosopher who has been frequently compared to satirists is Diogenes the Cynic (Condren, 2012, p. 383), who was famous for his 'fearless acts of truth telling (*parrhēsia*)' (Branham Bracht, 2009, pp. 146–147). According to Peter Sloterdijk (1987), Diogenes exhibited a 'satirical intelligence' which he identifies as *kynicism* – to distinguish it from cynicism in its modern sense (p. 287).

Several scholars have drawn on Sloterdijk's kynicism to frame the critical function of contemporary satire like *The Simpsons* (Gray, 2005, p. 154), *The Thick of It* (Higgie, 2014) and *The Colbert Report* (Jones, 2010, pp. 246–251). However, Sloterdijk (1987) argues that 'what we in our scientific tradition call "critique" is nothing other than a satirical function that no longer understands itself' (p. 287) and adds that '[t]he critical addiction to making things better has to be given up' (p. xxxvii). Instead Sloterdijk (1987) advocates that 'we cannot be nihilistic enough' (p. 541) and promotes a 'cosmic passivity' or 'a letting happen' (p. 540). For this reason, Sloterdijk's kynicism is ultimately not the most apt model to frame the critical purpose of contemporary satire.

Moreover, there are significant differences between satire and philosophy in general (Diehl, 2013). Still, in a looser sense, these comparisons are useful because they rightfully highlight the existential and moral dimension of satire as critique. At least in part, satire is driven by an existential concern to redress injustice and improve wellbeing. This existential concern is fundamentally moral. According to Simon Blackburn (1998), the moral domain starts when we are no longer happy to agree to disagree but take a stand in opposition to that with which we disagree (p. 8). As critique, satire consists exactly of such moral opposition to social wrongness. As James Sutherland (1958) argues, it is 'the mark of the satirist that he [*sic.*] cannot accept and refuses to tolerate' and is 'driven to protest' (p. 4).

Often, satirical critique opposes grave social injustice. Consider Spike Lee's *BlacKkKlansman*, which critiques white supremacism and the complacency which has allowed it to thrive in contemporary times. Yet, satirical critique can also target more trivial wrongness, like when the creators of *South Park* satirised a common conflation between their own '[d]eep, situational and emotional jokes' and the comedy of *Family Guy*, which they dismissed as 'one interchangeable joke after another' (Parker & Stone, 2006). Although such conflation is hardly the gravest injustice, *South Park*'s satire functions as critique because its creators are unwilling to let it slide.

The difference between *South Park* and *Family Guy* is also relevant to distinguish satirical critique from shock comedy. Although not everyone agrees (Peterson, 2008, *passim*), scholars have defended *South Park*'s deliberately transgressive comedy as a 'satiric attack' which aims at 'correction and change' (Stratyner & Keller, 2009, p. 3). The transgressions of *Family Guy* and its creator, Seth MacFarlane, have similarly been defended in the name of satire (DeRochi, 2008). However, critics have dismissed such defences on the grounds that

> *[s]atire is meant to take one thing and examine it through a humorous lens, usually in a critical way. MacFarlane's humor often doesn't have that object at all – it's one-dimensional shock humor. (MacDonald, 2013)*

Take MacFarlane's controversial performance as host of the 2013 Oscars, where he clearly set out to offend. His most controversial skit was a song called 'We Saw Your Boobs!' (MacFarlane, 2013). In the song, MacFarlane introduced films in which actresses like Meryl Streep, Naomi Watts and Halle Berry were naked, gleefully stating that seeing their breasts 'made us feel excited and alive'. MacFarlane clearly revelled in the knowledge that his performance was deliberately offensive. The skit was introduced by *Star Trek*'s Captain Kirk, who had travelled 'back in time from the 23rd century to stop [MacFarlane] from destroying the Academy Awards'. Kirk confronted MacFarlane with next day's headlines, which branded him as 'Worst Oscar host ever' and warned him about singing 'an incredibly offensive song that upsets a lot of actresses in the audience'.

Ironically, MacFarlane responded with surprise and indignation when his performance received the expected backlash he so clearly cultivated. He argued that his skit

> *was presented as part of an alternate universe where everything at the Oscars was done incorrectly, [but] the media ignored the context entirely. Comedy and satire being treated with more outrage than* actual *sexism, racism, or homophobia makes no sense at all. (Radloff, 2014, original emphasis)*

Similarly, the producers of the Oscars argued that '[e]veryone who complained missed the joke, it was satire' and added that '[w]e live in a society that is not very conscious of satire anymore' (Zakari, 2013).

However, critics denied that MacFarlane's performance lived up to that 'high concept' satire and urged him to stop complaining and 'transform his work into the highbrow satire he so emptily maintains that it is' (Donnelly, 2014). Such critics maintain that MacFarlane's shock comedy lacked the moral purpose of satire as critique, despite his appropriation of the label. Indeed, although MacFarlane clearly revelled in his reputation as an offensive comedian, it is less clear that his cultivated offensiveness at the Oscar ceremony served a serious critical purpose.

Such misappropriation of the label 'satire' to justify shock comedy is common. Take the Dutch broadcaster Jan Roos, who ran for office in The Netherlands in 2017, but was most known for a comedy routine which involved insulting people at public events. Critics have accused him of sexism and harassment. For example, he once revelled in mock indignation when a woman berated him for groping her breasts on national television. In defence, Roos (2017) argued that 'I played a character in a satirical show' (my translation). Similarly, when the Belgian columnist Herman Brusselmans called the Dutch singer-songwriter Anouk, who has six children, 'a blond slut who refuses to swallow the pill', his lawyer argued that 'Brusselmans writes satire' which means 'you exaggerate' (Cardoen, 2017, my translation).

Such conflations between satire and shock comedy are pernicious. Satire is often transgressive, but always has a moral purpose to attack social wrongness. By contrast, shock comedy just transgresses for the sake of it. When Brusselmans called Anouk a slut because she has six children, it was not to advance an argument about the need to control the growth of the human population. He simply sought to offend. By contrast, satire incorporates a serious purpose to critique perceived social wrongness, sustained by an analysis to expose that wrongness. Such morally serious considerations are absent from shock comedy.

However, although satire involves moral seriousness, it is not necessarily morally right. For one, the sexual politics of Roman satirists are deeply problematic, as when Juvenal (2004) attacks the 'injustices of Rome' and exclaims, '[w]hen a womanly eunuch takes a wife! (...) then it is hard *not* to write satire' (p. 133, original emphasis). Satire is not by default on the side of the good. In the early days of the German Reich, leading Nazi radio broadcaster Hans Fritzsche (1934) commended Joseph Goebbles for drawing 'from humor the sharpness of irony (...) [a]nd satire, too (...) which drove many an opponent to lose his head'. Such morally disturbing satire has recently resurfaced in the form of racist and antisemitic memes on Neo-Nazi and alt-right internet fora.

Hence, the label 'satire' is not necessarily a moral badge of honour. Yet, even morally bad satire has a serious moral purpose that is absent from more puerile forms of comedy. News parody and faux news websites like *The Onion* in the US and *The Daily Mash* in the UK are often marketed and received as satire, while they mostly poke fun at current affairs rather than seriously critique it. The same goes for topical comedy shows like *Mock the Week* in the UK or *De Ideale Wereld* (*The Ideal World*) in Belgium, which use politics as a resource for comedy. Scholars like Russell Peterson have, therefore, argued that there is a distinction between 'comedy *about* politics' and 'genuine satire, which uses comedic means to advance a serious critique' (Peterson, 2008, p. 9, original emphasis).

This distinction also matters to satirists themselves. When accepting the Herblock Prize for editorial cartooning, Jen Sorensen (2014) inscribed her work in Herblock's satirical tradition by explaining that 'he drew from a clear moral perspective' and did not 'go for innocuous, crowd-pleasing Jay Leno-style gags'. Similarly, another Herblock awardee, Dan Perkins (aka Tom Tomorrow) (2016), took offense at *Dilbert*'s common reception as satire, because it 'had a reputation as a critique of corporate power, when in reality it was just a comic strip about the banalities of office life' (p. 316).

Conflating satire with more puerile and trivial forms of comedy obscures the moral seriousness and existential significance of the genre. Such conflations stand in the way of appreciating how satire can offer interesting insights into experiences of mental health and even serve as a resource to maintain good mental health in a challenging socio-political environment. Satire's concern for wellbeing in a social context means that the genre introduces serious existential reflection. In this sense, satirists are like philosophers who set out to improve their own wellbeing and that of others. Granted, not all satirists do so explicitly, nor always in a way that we can morally endorse, but the genre's moral seriousness and existential significance does distinguish it from shock humour and topical comedy.

ENTERTAINMENT

At the same time, satire is not exhausted by moral seriousness. Satire does not just critique, but it also entertains. In this respect, satirists are rather different from philosophers (see Diehl, 2013). Their job is not simply to stimulate existential reflection, but also, in equal part, to promote a good time. This combination of critique and entertainment is what makes satire so distinct, because although these two purposes fruitfully interact, they do ultimately pull in different directions. Specifically, there is a risk that the aesthetic concerns involved in entertainment distract from the serious moral concerns associated with critique. This tension is what Atwood (2012) calls the genre's 'doubleness', which explains its ambiguous reception.

I will develop a detailed understanding of entertainment in Chapter 4, when I investigate its coping affordances. For now, I introduce some basic ideas about the nature of entertainment to clarify its productive, yet ambiguous interaction with critique in satire. Entertainment is characterised by three fundamental dimensions. The first is a functional dimension of diversion, that is, an anti-seriousness that distinguishes it from the serious business of everyday life (Shusterman, 2003, p. 292). Entertainment is what we do 'for fun'. Second, entertainment involves an emotional dimension associated with uncomplicated pleasures; in a word, entertainment is 'fun' (Robinson & Knobloch-Westerwick, 2016). Third, entertainment's social dimension is characterised by a low status, in contrast to more serious art (Dyer, 1992, p. 2). These three dimensions of entertainment also characterise satire.

The idea that satirists are 'entertainers' is well established (Griffin, 1994, p. 75). Since Roman times, satire has traditionally been situated in a 'context of festivity, [as] an occasion marked off from business for the play of wit' (Griffin, 1994, p. 84; see also Habinek, 2005). Satire has equally been associated with aesthetic pleasure, as 'we may be sure that writing their satires never caused [satirists] pain. They have enjoyed it; and we enjoy what they have written' (Grigson, 1980, p. v). Finally, satire has since antiquity been presented and received in various contexts as lowbrow, even if many satires are now canonical (Highet, 1962, p. 3; Hodgart, 1969, p. 10; Jones, 2007, p. 1; Kernan, 1959, p. 17; Meijer Drees, & Nieuwenhuis, 2010, p. 198; Nokes, 1987, p. 8; Wight, 1964 [1936], p. 6).

Since entertainment is central to satire, some have argued that satire is amoral (Griffin, 1994). However, as discussed, the moral seriousness of critique is what sets satire apart from certain kinds of comedy, which are arguably 'just' entertainment. Instead, I agree with those who have framed satire as a combination of critique and entertainment, in various formulations. Scholars have called satire 'a weapon and a toy' (Nokes, 1987, p. 17), which is situated between 'jest and earnest' (Highet, 1962, p. 233) and 'aims to entertain and amuse as well as to inform and reform' (Brown, 1993, p. 3) or 'to sting and amuse' (Wight, 1964 [1936], p. 9).

Satire's moral purpose to critique and aesthetic purpose to entertain fruitfully interact. Berys Gaut discusses the example of Lenny Henry ridiculing the anti-immigration policy of a British Prime Minister by quipping 'Enoch Powell wants to give black people a thousand pounds to go back home, which suits me fine – it only costs me 20p on the bus' (quoted in Gaut, 1998, p. 66). According to Gaut (1998), 'the [aesthetic] effectiveness and resonance of the joke centrally depend on its subversion of racist attitudes and assumptions' (p. 66). In other words, the joke is funny, because it is critical.

Similarly, Robert Stecker (2010) argues that interaction can also happen the other way around by highlighting that

> *to satirize a questionable aspect of society (...) [audiences] must be able to* feel *by way of vividly imaging (...) the folly of the satirized aspect of society or the bad consequences of the practice in need of reform.' (pp. 210–211, original emphasis)*

Here the aesthetic force of vivid imagination contributes to the moral dismissal of social wrongness.

The interaction between satire's moral and aesthetic purposes is captured by the seventeenth-century rhetorician Joshua Poole (1657), who compiled a list of adjectives that were commonly associated with satire, including 'biting, snarling, scourging, jerking, lashing, smarting, sharp, tart, rough, (...), whipping, thorny, pricking, stinging, sharp-fanged' (p. 176). Clearly, qualities like 'sharpness' or 'bitingness' can be appreciated for both moral and aesthetic reasons.

Such value interaction still characterises contemporary criticism of satire. In her review of *The Handmaid's Tale*, Joyce Carol Oates (2006) argues that '[n]arrated in the breathless present tense (...) *The Handmaid's Tale* achieves the feat of rendering the bizarre, the ludicrous, and the improbable a new sort of quotidian'. In similar vein, she lauds Atwood for including a 'startling appendix' which 'makes of the novel an astute, provocative social commentary' (Oates, 2006). Oates's point is that certain aesthetic qualities which make *The Handmaid's Tale* an entertaining novel also substantiate its moral value as critique (by substantiating its insightfulness).

This interaction between the moral purpose of critique and the aesthetic purpose of entertainment explains why humour is such a central feature of satire (and why many satires are hybrid comedies). We find something funny because it presents a deviation from how 'we think the world is or should be' (Carroll, 2014, p. 17; see also Chapter 5). Such incongruities are not only entertaining but can also 'function to *enforce* norms – to serve as a corrective' (Carroll, 2014, p. 76, original emphasis). Satire's use of humour is enforcing in this way by targeting social wrongness.

Nevertheless, satire is not always funny – just consider Orwell's *1984* (Condren, 2012, p. 389). Similarly, Jimi Hendrix's satirical adaptation of *The Star-Spangled Banner* at Woodstock is not amusing, nor is it designed to be. In his virtuosic guitar solo, Hendrix mangles and distorts the sounds of the American national anthem to evoke the sound of exploding bombs – as a critique on the Vietnam War. Still, Hendrix's virtuosic performance fruitfully interacts with the entertainment of a rock concert. Hence, alongside an impulse to critique, what matters for satire is not necessarily that it is funny, but that it entertains.

Moreover, it is equally crucial that satire's purposes to critique and entertain are not subordinate to each other (even if they fruitfully interact). Hendrix is at least as interested in critiquing the Vietnam War as he is in showing off his guitar skills for our aesthetic appreciation. In other words, satire is not critique *through* entertainment, because satirists do not just entertain to support their critique. They also entertain for the sake of it. Consider *Last Week Tonight with John Oliver*. Although praised for its journalistic critique, Oliver has always downplayed 'any larger sense of mission', explaining that the show is 'so clearly comedy' (Marchese, 2016).

According to Sophia McClennen (2016), such disavowals are just a pragmatic way for satirists to slip their critique under the radar by claiming that 'they are just entertainers'. For one, disavowing journalistic status permits satirists to pursue critique without having to live up to all the norms of investigative journalism (Declercq, 2019). Nonetheless, satirists like Oliver are also sincere when claiming that they spend considerable resources on entertainment for the sake of it.

For example, Oliver (2019) once set out to embarrass the authoritarian President of Turkmenistan, Gurbanguly Berdimuhamedow, by commissioning 'the world's largest marble cake featuring an image of him falling of a horse'. Berdimuhamedow has somewhat of a fascination with collecting Guinness World Records, so the project was also a satire of that company's proclivity to validate the megalomania of authoritarian leaders. Yet, actually going ahead and baking a 600-square feet cake does not really foster the purpose of critique – at the very least, it is a very inefficient allocation of resources (even if leftovers were donated to charity). Instead, as Oliver puts it, he indulges in these projects because what 'we get really excited about' is 'the spectacle' (Marchese, 2016).

Satire's indulgence in entertainment for its own sake contrasts with other critical art, like the graphic art of Stephanie McMillan. McMillan started her career drawing a satirical comic strip called *Minimum Security*, which critics praised as '[r]azor-sharp critique packaged as cute-kid-and-funny-animal cartoon' (Booklist Staff, 2007) and 'social satire at its wittiest and most engaging' (Howard Zinn quoted in Seven Stories Staff, 2013). However, over the years, McMillan's (2015) output has ceased to be entertaining in its own right. This development culminated in a series of graphic work for a book entitled *Capitalism Must Die!*. Published by an independent Marxist collective, *Capitalism Must Die!* incorporates didactic diagrams and lengthy prose which lack the dimension of entertainment for its own sake, essential to satire.

McMillan acknowledges that her graphic work is not 'art-for-arts-sake' but instead instrumental to 'social change' (Leonard, 2015). She explains that 'colourful graphics help draw readers in to give longer texts a chance, which they otherwise might avoid as potentially boring' (Leonard, 2015). Since she considers her artistic practice as a 'tool' in the service of a Marxist critique, McMillan's graphic work has gradually moved from a satirical combination of critique and entertainment to the straightforward didacticism of *Capitalism Must Die!* (Leonard, 2015). By contrast, satire does not just entertain for the sake of critique, but also in its own right.

The upshot is that artists who are only devoted to critique ultimately seem to gravitate away from satire. When stand-up comedian Dick Gregory became increasingly involved as an activist in the civil rights movement, he left the showbiz of satire in favour of directly activist strategies such as hunger strikes and political rallies (Nachman, 2003, pp. 494–508). As an instrument to critique, Gregory found entertainment wanting, arguing that '[h]umor can no more find the solution to race problems than it can cure cancer. We didn't laugh Hitler out of existence' (quoted in Nachman, 2003, p. 501). By contrast, satirists seem happy to devote some of their resources to entertainment for its own sake, for if they were only interested in critique, they would likely opt for more direct forms of political action.

AMBIGUITY

Satire's pursuit of entertainment for its own sake makes it ambiguous as a form of critique. Although satire's moral purpose to critique interacts fruitfully with its aesthetic purpose to entertain, they do ultimately pull in different directions. On the one hand, critique is a moral task that demands that we spend resources to redress social wrongness. On the other hand, entertainment is something we do for fun and involves the leisurely enjoyment of aesthetic pleasures. This ambiguity between critique and entertainment makes satire distinct.

The tension between moral and aesthetic purposes is more pronounced in satire than other critical art. Consider, Ai Weiwei's *Straight*, an installation which repurposes mangled steel rods from poorly built schools that were destroyed during an earthquake. Resembling the undulated surface of a fault in the earth's crust, the 90-ton steel structure serves to indict a lack of foresight and poor planning, but also invites aesthetic appreciation of its physical and emotional magnitude. Yet, *Straight* is hardly an artwork we would engage with for fun. In the words of one curator,

> *it is a very sombre and sobering work when you see it, it has this kind of power and silence about it ... it bears a real sense of loss of life. (Brown, 2015)*

Similarly, although we can imagine tourists leisurely appreciating Picasso's *Guernica,* as they amble around the Museo Reina Sofía in Madrid on a sunny day, something is clearly missing from their appreciation. Certainly, *Guernica* invites appreciation of its artistic ingenuity and inventiveness. But its portrayal of suffering people and animals distorted in violent chaos, which represents the real bombing of the Basque town Guernica, does not set out to provide leisurely enjoyment. Instead, we should be deeply moved by *Guernica* and our aesthetic appreciation of the painting should be characterised by solemnity, not fun.

By contrast, central to our appreciation of satire is that it should be enjoyable and something we do for fun. For this reason, satire is much more ambiguous than other critical art. A particularly striking example of this ambiguity is a comic poem by the German comedian Jan Böhmermann, about the Turkish President Erdogan, which caused a storm in European politics. The poem was a response to the Turkish government's demand to impose a ban on an earlier satirical song produced by the German TV show *extra 3*.

The original satire by *extra 3* critiqued the Erdogan regime for limiting press freedom, disavowing gender equality, and perpetrating human rights offences. Whereas Turkey requested that the German government ban the song, the German ambassador in Ankara instead affirmed the protection of political satire in Germany under the right to freedom of speech and freedom of media (Zeit Staff, 2016). In response, Böhmermann ridiculed Erdogan's peevishness with an ironically offensive poem in his show *Neo Magazin Royale*. This time, however, the German government did allow the prosecution of the comedian (Spiegel Staff, 2016) and Böhmermann was ultimately prohibited to repeat most lines of the poem (Zeit Staff, 2016).

The poem was part of a larger skit that ridiculed Erdogan's response to *extra 3*'s satire. At the start, Böhmermann mock-seriously explained to 'Herr Erdogan' that satirical critique was legal in Europe's liberal democracies. However, he soon moved on to a discussion of *Schmähkritik*, a judicial term introduced in German legislation exactly to penalise cases in which freedom of speech turned into libel. In a poem cheekily entitled 'Schmähkritik', Böhmermann (2016a) then set out to do exactly the forbidden.

In his 'Schmähkritik', Böhmermann rhymed various insults together, among other things calling Erdogan a goatfucker, woman beater and paedophile. His performance also ironically alluded to various existing racist and xenophobic stereotypes about Turkish people in German society. All the while, he kept his audience in the loop of his ironic joke, mock-seriously highlighting that publicising such a poem would be illegal in Germany (joking that if one nonetheless were to do so, the performance might even be deleted from the broadcaster's online media library!).

The satirical status of Böhmermann's performance is ambiguous. Böhmermann has alternated between describing his poem as a 'humorous university seminar' and a 'fart joke' (Ebel, 2016, my translation). He has also described himself as both a 'mischievous joker' (*Spaßvogel*) and someone whose critical task is 'to ask questions, kick off debates and raise issues' (Kalle & von Uslar, 2016, my translation). In this respect, while Böhmermann fulminated that critics had taken his poem out of context and consequently missed the point, he continually sent mixed messages about his own aims.

Intriguingly, *Neo Magazin Royale* is marketed as 'satire', but Böhmermann explicitly disavowed the satirical status of his programme throughout the episode. Contrasting *Neo Magazin Royale* to *extra 3* (which originally satirised Erdogan), Böhmermann (2016a) explicitly stated that '[w]e are in the broadest sense not a satire programme, we are more a *Quatsch* [nonsense] programme' (my translation). Later, he again stressed that *Neo Magazin Royale* is 'Germany's number one *Quatsch* programme. That's us. We have nothing to do with satire' (my translation). Böhmermann also ironically contended that *Neo Magazin Royale* does not aim to tackle such difficult issues as *extra 3* – which his sidekick, Jan Kabelka, wholeheartedly endorsed.

However, when retrospectively defending the democratic significance of *Neo Magazin Royale*, Böhmermann (2016b) did embrace the label 'satire', contending that 'my team and I have made it our mission in the past three years to satirically tackle the top issues in politics, TV and gossip' (my translation). In conclusion, throughout his performance, but also afterwards, Böhmermann was not only ambivalent about the purpose of his performance, but also its status as satire. Therefore, it is difficult to tell whether Böhmermann's *Schmähkritik* is really satire or shock comedy.

Such ambiguity about the satirical status of a performance is relatively exceptional. While MacFarlane was quick to resort to the label 'satire' in defence of his performance at the Oscars, there was nothing genuinely critical about 'We Saw Your Boobs!' MacFarlane (2013) was clearly taking cheap shots, as when he started his speech by introducing *Django Unchained* as 'the story of a man fighting to get back his woman, who's been subjected to unthinkable violence. Or as Chris Brown and Rhianna call it, a date movie'. By contrast, Böhmermann's performance is so ambiguous because it is not clear whether he transgresses for a political purpose or just for the sake of it.

Nevertheless, while the ambiguity of *Schmähkritik* is exceptional, it does highlight that satire is itself ambiguous. Despite its flippancy, Böhmermann's performance *could* be satire – because entertainment is central to the genre and flippancy is often entertaining. Thus, Böhmermann's performance signals an important ambiguity in satire's combination of critique and entertainment. Although satire's aesthetic purpose to entertain typically supports its moral purpose to critique, it also risks undermining it.

Satire's ambiguity is well established in scholarship. Marijke Meijer Drees and Ivo Nieuwenhuis (2010) identify a 'diffuse boundary between seriousness and amusement' in satire, which 'introduces a tension' (p. 201, my translation). Similarly, Niyi Akingbe (2014) discusses a tension between satire's 'requirements of aesthetic satisfaction and social relevance' (pp. 65–66). Some, like Lisa Colletta (2009), therefore wonder if the 'social and political satire of television shows such as *The Daily Show*, *The Colbert Report*, and *The Simpsons* really have any kind of efficacy beyond that of mere entertainment?' (p. 859). It is to these concerns about the political impact of satire that I turn next.

CONCLUSION

Satire is a genre with the purpose to critique and entertain (with the qualification that these purposes interact, although neither is wholly instrumental to the other). Crucially, satire is not simply critique *through* entertainment, because satirists also just entertain for the sake of it. This dimension of entertainment for its own sake does make satire ambiguous as a form of critique, especially in contrast to other forms of critical art. Yet, in the rest of this book, I argue that satire's ambiguity is not an obstacle that needs to be overcome to defend the genre's significance. Instead, I argue that satire's ambiguity affords valuable coping in a depressing socio-political environment. In the next chapter, I pre-empt the worry that such coping automatically means that satire can have no political impact as critique.

2

SATIRE AS THERAPY: CURING A SICK WORLD?

INTRODUCTION

This chapter investigates and reassesses the idea of satire as therapy. There is a common conception of satire as a therapy for the socio-political ills of the world. I criticise this conception as too 'heroic' because it unduly frames the satirist as a political hero who changes the world through satire. I do not deny that satire has political affordances, but these should not be overstated, nor should the real significance of the genre be framed in terms of political impact. If satire has political affordances, these should be primarily conceptualised as harnessing emotional resources to stimulate or sustain other forms of political action, which have greater political impact. To philosophically ground these political affordances of satire, I introduce R. G. Collingwood's (1938) theory of 'magic' representations.

HEROIC THERAPY

The idea that satire functions as a therapy that heals socio-political illness has long been commonplace in criticism and scholarship. In antiquity, Roman satirists defended satire as a rhetorical cure for moral flaws (Kivistö, 2009, p. 13). Modern scholars equally adopt this medical conception. Alvin Kernan (1959) argues that, for Juvenal, 'the case of man and society is desperate, and he applies appropriate therapeutic treatments: the whip, the scalpel, the strappado, the emetic, the burning acid' (p. 22). Similarly, John Wight (1964 [1936]) explains that, for satirists like Horace, 'satire is a literary medicine for a world morally and socially out of health; and, if this holds good, the satirist is a kind of doctor' (p. 8).

The argument goes that satire is

> *a bitter but necessary medicine for a society that wants to cure itself from all sorts of social and moral ills, and the satirist is the doctor who delivers this medicine as a cure to the patient, the target of the satire. (Meijer Drees & Nieuwenhuis, 2010, p. 209, my translation)*

This conception of satire as a punitive but curative practice became increasingly prominent during the early modern period (Randolph, 1941). Early modern satirists and critics presented satire 'as a kind of medicine for the mind or soul, designed to treat moral corruption in much the same way that a course of physic could treat bodily illness' (Gallagher, 2013). Just consider William Combe's (1777) appraisal of the satirist, who 'with matchless skill, employs the knife, whose wholesome wound preserves the patient's life' (p. 21).

This medical conception of satire as a punitive therapy has clear heroic overtones. Early modern satirists and critics even argued that 'no remedy is more effective in curing social ills than satire' (Elkin 1973, p. 74). Similarly, in the early twentieth century, the German critic Kurt Tucholsky (1919) argued that social 'malice' like alcoholism must be combatted 'by grippingly representing a hopeless drunk. I pull the curtain, which was gently spread over the foulness, and say: "Look!"' (my translation). Tucholsky (1919) appeals to the enduring idea of satire as a curative and punitive practice when he argues that 'alcohol addiction is a nasty thing. It damages society, and only the merciless truth can come to the rescue' (my translation).

Tucholsky does lament that the establishment often mistakes satire's punitive truth-telling for 'crassness' (Tucholsky, 1919). His defence of satire remains influential today, especially in Germany. When Jan Böhmermann faced legal prosecution for reciting a derogatory poem about the Turkish President Erdogan (see Chapter 1), prominent German publisher Mathias Döpfner (2016) defended his actions in the 'tradition of freedom of speech, artistic freedom and satirical freedom, shaped by Tucholsky'. According to Döpfner (2016), Böhmermann's crassness was necessary 'to provoke people to the highest possible degree'. In other words, the satirist must display a heroic courage to speak truth and transgress established norms to cure socio-political malice. Such heroic transgression is what the English satirist Tony Hendra (1987) has colloquially called 'going too far'.

Satire's licence for punitive transgression is often justified not only by analogies to medicine, but also philosophy (see Chapter 1). Robert Bracht Branham (2009) argues that what philosophers and satirists have in common is '[e]vidently, the willingness to offend, provoke, and outrage, all in the name of calling a spade a bloody shovel, of telling the awful truth' (p. 140). Similarly, Sari Kivistö (2009) argues that in Roman antiquity, 'satirical therapy' involved 'treatments that can be seen as playful and rhetorical versions of philosophical remedies' (p. 171).

The heroic conception of the satirist as philosopher has remained influential in modern times. When Lenny Bruce died, aged 40, in the wake of a high-profile conviction for obscenity, a process of 'deification' started which solidified his image as a 'heroic figure' (Ebert, 1974). Julian Barry (1971) wrote a Broadway play, *Lenny*, in which he explicitly inscribed Bruce in a tradition of philosophical heroism. In the preface to the script of the play, Barry drew an explicit parallel between the trials of Lenny Bruce and Socrates, who were both wrongly sentenced to death by 'idiots' (Shaw cited in Barry, 1971, p. v). Ingmar Bergman alluded to similar ideas when stating that Bruce's 'only offence was that he dared to tell people the truth' (Bergman in Cohen, 1975, p. 1).

This heroic conception is still prominent in contemporary scholarship. Stephen E. Kercher (2006) argues that American satirists in the 1960s, including Lenny Bruce, were committed to 'brutal truth' and 'terrible honesty' (p. 78). Geoffrey Baym praises contemporary satirists like Jon Stewart and Stephen Colbert as political heroes who, during the presidency of George W. Bush, dared to reveal 'a truth the mainstream media were largely refusing to consider' (2010, p. 167; see also Jones, 2010, p. 168). Similarly, Russell Peterson (2008) argues that 'if "speaking truth to power" is part of the journalist's job, it is the satirist's primary mission – a higher calling, in fact, than merely being funny' (p. 8).

Contemporary heroic appraisals of satire sometimes still evoke medical language, especially the idea that satire is good for the 'health' of democracy (McClennen & Maisel, 2014, p. 200). For example, Owen Jones (2014), columnist in *The Guardian*, argues that '[t]here's nothing the establishment hates more than ridicule – that's why it's vital for a healthy democracy'. Moreover, even when contemporary heroic appraisals of satire do not explicitly use medical analogies, they often do reiterate its professed punitive effects. For example, scholars have called satire 'a *hard-knuckled* critique of power' (Jones, 2010, p. 83, my emphasis) or a '*stinging* critique in the guise of good humor' (Baym, 2010, p. 124, my emphasis).

Outside academia, these heroic appraisals are often turned up a notch. In clickbait journalism, satire's effects are often framed as not just punitive, but deadly. In the run-up to the 2016 American presidential elections, critics regularly recommended readers to watch videos of John Oliver 'annihilate'

(Reed, 2016), 'murderslay' (Magary, 2016) or 'absolutely destroy' Donald Trump (SW Staff, 2019). What's particularly puzzling is that these claims about satire's professed 'deadliness' were still common after Trump took office as US President (Dessem, 2017; Juntwait, 2017). Given that all the satire in the world did not keep Trump out of the White House in 2016, these heroic claims about the political impact of the genre seem doubtful.

POLITICAL IMPACT

Supporters of satire have often made heroic claims about the genre's political impact. For example, Sophia McClennen (2011) argues that 'satire is an extremely effective form of political critique' (p. 97), while Owen Jones (2014) states that '[s]atire is so subversive – and often politically fatal for those who rule – because it exposes the absurdities of power'. However, empirical research into satire's political effects has been inconclusive. Surveying over a decade's worth of research, R. Lance Holbert (2013) concluded that 'there is no clear evidence that political satire use is necessarily good or bad for democracy' (p. 312), adding that, '[a]t best, the persuasive effects of political satire appear to be minimal' (p. 310). Similarly, Dannagal Young (2018) argues that satire's 'impact on knowledge, attitudes, and behaviors is far from clear' (p. 879).

In response, scholars like Holbert and Young have proposed that the political effects of satire are too subtle to be measured using traditional parameters. Instead, we should expand our understanding of satire's political effects beyond easily measurable outcomes, like salience, knowledge, attitudes and political behaviour, to include more subtle outcomes, like joy, enthusiasm, curiosity and an inner sense of political engagement (Young, Holbert, & Jamieson, 2014, pp. 1112–1117). Likewise, Amber Day (2011, pp. 21–23, 2013, p. 427) argues that scholars should investigate the incremental shifts and changes that contemporary satire achieves in public debates, which, she grants, are difficult to measure empirically. Along the same lines, Sophie Quirk (2015) concedes that '[t]he contribution that most comedians make to social change is, perhaps, more ethereal' (p. 203).

These concessions signal an important ambiguity in contemporary scholarship about satire. Contemporary supporters of satire largely dismiss the heroic conception that satire, by itself, cures socio-political sickness; instead, they stress that audiences also need to engage in political action (Baym, 2009, p. 150; Gray, 2005, p. 168; Jones, 2010, p. 39; McClennen, 2011, p. 181). Amber Day (2011) explicitly dismisses the idea that satire 'could or should be expected to single-handedly cause quantifiable political change' as 'almost absurd' (p. 137). And yet, as is clear from the survey above, a certain sense of heroism does still permeate contemporary scholarship on satire.

Sometimes, the underlying heroism is subtle, and lurks in paratexts, as on the cover of Day's *Satire and Dissent* (2011), where a steady hand pricks American Flag balloons with a sharp needle – as an allusion to satire's destructive force. Sometimes, the heroism is more forcefully expressed, as when Baym (2009) calls satire 'a new kind of democratic activism' which is 'beholden to none of the paradigmatic conventions that limit the effectiveness of much contemporary journalism [in the US post-9/11]' (p. 167). Similarly, McClennen and Maisel (2014) argue that, after 9/11, satire 'emerged as one of the strongest voices of critical thought and democratic deliberation' (p. 6).

A plausible reason why supporters of satire, who are aware of the genre's limited political impact, fall back on a certain heroism in their appraisals is because there are sceptics who deny the political impact of satire altogether or frame it exclusively in negative terms (Hart, 2013; Webber, 2013). Such scepticism is often informed by the Frankfurt School's distrust of the culture industry, according to which complicity in capitalism prevents meaningful political impact (see Adorno & Horkheimer, 2002 [1944]). As entertainment, contemporary satire is often mainstream, commercial and popular. This commercial complicity raises suspicions about satire's professed mission to 'speak truth to power' when it is often so closely entwined with the mechanisms of power in a capitalist marketplace.

In response, Jonathan Gray (2005) proposes that commercial satire needs to strike a 'Faustian bargain' with media conglomerates to secure a wide platform for its critical message (pp. 164–165). He likens the relationship between complicit satirists and their powerful targets to the fool's jokes at the expense of the king at medieval courts (Gray, 2005, pp. 11–12). This solution strikes me as essentially right because it grants that satire has political affordances, without overstating them. Gray (2005) is also right to argue that when progressive impulses and conservative realities clash, the latter do not necessarily prevail over the former (p. 167). In this respect, Michael Moore quips that '[o]ne of the beauties of capitalism is that they'll sell you the rope to hang themselves if they believe that they can make money' (quoted in Jones, 2010, p. 156).

However, sceptics may be less convinced by Gray's fool and king analogy, which echoes Mikhail Bakhtin's ideas about medieval carnival as a time and space for the inversion of official norms (see Stam, 1989). Umberto Eco (1984) dismisses the authorised and institutionalised transgression of the carnival as a conservative tool to maintain the status quo. Similarly, other sceptics dismiss satirists as 'ersatz activist[s]' (Hart, 2013, p. 340) and satire as 'a conservative, relief-inducing way of maintaining the status quo' (Webber, 2013, p. 147).

Recent debates about satire, especially in media and communication studies, have been animated by such back and forth about the professed political impact of the genre. Although these debates have certainly helped to refine our understanding of satire, they may never be fruitfully resolved because of how difficult it is to empirically establish the political impact of satire. Unpacking the complex networks of causal connections between the production and consumption of satire, on the one hand, and political consequences, on the other hand, will most likely forever prove elusive.

Moreover, I also do not think that satire's significance should be framed primarily in terms of political impact. This focus is too narrow and overlooks other ways in which satire can be (more) significant. Instead, I propose that satire's real significance lies in its contribution to sustaining mental health in a troubled socio-political world – a proposal which I develop in the next chapters. Yet, to pre-empt concerns that satire, therefore, stimulates political apathy, I first argue that satire does have genuine but modest political affordances, which I reframe in terms of 'magic'.

SATIRE AS MAGIC

Satire's political impact is difficult to measure empirically. Therefore, philosophical explication is useful to establish what kind of political impact satire could have (and, equally importantly, *not* have). Perhaps surprisingly, the concept 'magic' is particularly useful to conceptually frame satire's political impact. According to R. G. Collingwood (1938), rather than pseudo-scientific sorcery, magic really consists of representations that harness emotional resources for their useful release in everyday life. Along these lines, I argue that satire has political affordances because it can emotionally stimulate or sustain more directly impactful forms of political action.

The connection between satire and magic in scholarship is well-established. Fred Norris Robinson (1912) argues that satirical verses in ancient Ireland functioned as 'magic spells' (p. 3). Irish satirists frequently referred to magic acts of 'blemishing', 'reddening' and 'cutting' the physical body with satirical curses (Robinson, 1912, p. 10). Similarly, legend has it that the archaic Greek poet Archilochus cursed his fiancée and her father into suicide with his satirical verses after they broke off an engagement (Elliott, 1960, p. 7). This magic belief that 'all satire "kills"' still lingers in heroic metaphorical descriptions of satire as 'venomous', 'cutting' and 'stinging' (Elliott, 1960, p. 4) – as well as claims that satirists 'murderslay' or 'destroy' their opponents.

Satire's magic power to harm, destroy or mutilate the physical body also informs the heroic conception of satire as therapy. Medical metaphors, which present satire as punitive but curative, shift the magic infliction of pain from the physical body to the soul, to stimulate moral healing (Randolph, 1941, p. 135). This pseudo-scientific foundation is even more reason to dismiss the heroic conception of satire as a cure for a sick world. Indeed, the idea that satire, by sheer representational force, destroys or cures its targets, surely belongs in the realm of wishful thinking.

Nonetheless, the connection between satire and magic should not be altogether dismissed as outdated superstition. According to Collingwood (1938), 'magic' really denotes a kind of representation, which, through media such as dance, song or drawing, seeks to arouse emotions for the useful release in everyday life (pp. 66–67). Through the representation of some practical situation, like defeating an enemy, magic primarily serves to harness the magician's own emotions to achieve a practical goal, such as waging war (Collingwood, 1938, pp. 66–67). Secondarily, a magic ritual also serves to boost the morale of a community who collectively pursue a practical goal as well as to damage the confidence of those who oppose that goal (Collingwood, 1938, p. 67).

A contemporary example of magic is the All Blacks' haka, the pre-match routine of the New Zealand rugby union team. Haka are Māori posture dances through which the rugby players symbolically display the strength that will deliver victory over their opponents. (For the purposes of my argument, I will sidestep the issue of whether this routine constitutes problematic cultural appropriation.) Before each game, the players gather in a formation and shout, stomp and slap in the direction of their opponents. In one controversial version, the *Kapa og Pango*, the players conclude their posture dance with a throat slitting gesture. The haka, as a magic ritual, serves two distinguishable purposes for the All Blacks. First, the performance gets the players (and their supporters) 'psyched up' for the game. Second, it intimidates the other team (and their supporters).

Professional sports are particularly fertile ground for contemporary magic. Before the 2009 UEFA Champions League final between FC Barcelona and Manchester United, which was held in Rome, the manager of the Spanish team screened a motivational video in the dressing room, which was especially produced for the occasion by Televisió de Catalunya (2009). The video juxtaposed shots from Ridley Scott's *Gladiator* with footage of the Barcelona team's performances earlier that year. The function of the video was essentially magic and served to motivate the players by representing the successful activities they needed to emulate for victory (from crucial saves to decisive goals). Further, it likened those activities on the pitch to the combat of victorious Roman gladiators, who slayed their enemies.

The All Black's haka and Barcelona's motivational video testify to the endurance of magic representations in contemporary culture. By representing victory over opponents, both representations emotionally prepare the players to outperform their competitors in the upcoming game. One notable difference is that the All Black's haka, as a public display, also serves to inspire fear in the opposition. Yet, neither representation suffices by itself to achieve victory, nor is it intended to do so. The All Blacks or the players of FC Barcelona obviously did not assume that they would no longer have to psychically exert themselves to achieve victory. Magic representations only aim to stir emotions, not to metaphysically generate the effects they represent through some supernatural process.

The emotional affordances of magic representations provide a fruitful model to reconceptualise the political affordances of satire. Satires are representations that critique social wrongness. They typically ridicule or otherwise attack represented targets. Satirical representations do not by themselves eradicate the social wrongness they target; satire is not in itself deadly for its targets, nor does it cure the moral sickness it exposes. Instead, if satire has political affordances, they should primarily be framed as magic, specifically harnessing emotional resources for political action. Foremost, satire serves to channel moral emotions like anger, disgust and contempt to support the political action of satirists and audiences. Secondarily, satire also emotionally impacts its targets, by frustrating, worrying or even shaming them. Yet, although these emotional affordances can have genuine political impact, this impact should not be overstated.

SATIRE AND TRUMP

The political affordances of satire as magic can be productively examined by considering satirical representations of Donald Trump. When Trump ran for President in 2016, and subsequently secured the White House, he was the target of much satire. The fact that he still became President is reason enough to abandon heroic conceptions about satire's political impact. Yet, granted that all the satire in the world cannot really 'murderslay' or 'destroy' Trump, the genre does have real political affordances, even if they are modest.

Satirists use representational strategies like ridicule to attack their targets. Sometimes, such ridicule echoes the destructive intentions of enchanter satirists like Archilochus. A good example of symbolically destructive satire is the representation of Donald Trump as a piñata, which has become a trope in Mexican and Hispanic culture. Apart from cartoons and memes which depict the battering of such piñatas, online retailers offer a varied selection of Trump-piñatas, while video-sharing websites host many clips of opponents smashing them at parties and protests.

These representations of Trump as a piñata serve to ridicule his image, by symbolically destroying it. Such a symbolic act strips Trump of his power, which is the ultimate political aim of these satirical practices. Therefore, making, sharing or laughing at such satirical representations always constitutes a political act at some level. However, what are the actual political effects of such satirical action?

If nothing else, satire can frustrate targets like Trump – as when he responded with anger on Twitter to Alec Baldwin's repeated impersonations on *Saturday Night Live* (Trump 2019). Still, satire's power to annoy Trump is hardly unique, as is clear from his trademark dismissal of news organisations like CNN and the *The New York Times* as 'fake news'. Moreover, although satirical representations may cause Trump to feel frustrated or angry, they hardly caused policy change, let alone terminated his Presidency.

Satire of Trump seems to have similar, equally modest effects on his supporters. When the American President visited the UK in 2018, protesters flew a giant Trump Baby blimp over Parliament Square in London. The blimp satirically represented Trump by depicting him as an angry, orange child, wearing a diaper and clutching his mobile phone as if it was a rattle. At the time, right-wing populist Nigel Farage was clearly annoyed by the protest and called it 'the biggest ever insult to a sitting president' (Lavelle, 2018).

When Trump revisited the UK a year later, and the blimp flew again, other Trump-supporters reacted with similar indignation. This time, protestors also devised a smaller blimp (Baby Trump Baby), which was stabbed with scissors by a pro-Trump activist and vlogger, who angrily called it 'a national disgrace', as she livestreamed her actions to her followers (Cambridge, 2019). Again, although the Trump Baby blimp clearly annoyed or upset some Trump supporters to the point of retaliation, it did not metaphorically 'destroy' or 'cure' them.

In fact, rather than 'destroying' or 'curing' political opponents, satire is more likely to deepen divisions. Consider Stephen Colbert's character Tuck Buckford, which satirises the style and politics of far-right conspiracy theorist, Alex Jones. In response, Jones (2017) dressed up as the 'real' Tuck Buckford, an angry liberal who ironically accused 'that enemy of America', Alex Jones, of stealing his persona, in order 'to spread his evil lies across the country and the world'. Jones (2017), as the 'real' Tuck Buckford, then whacked a Trump-piñata with a small axe, shouting 'this isn't violent at all', before ripping its head off, which he justified as 'liberal' and 'open'. Unsurprisingly, Jones's satire was in turn ridiculed by the liberals he targeted, thus, only spurring on a continuing cycle of political antagonism (Pennacchia, 2017).

Although satire can have an emotional impact on its targets, it falls short of changing or weakening their political positions; if anything, it often seems to strengthen those positions. The limited effects of satire on the practical goals which it represents are consistent with the affordances of magic representations. The emotional impact of magic is only secondarily aimed to detriment its targets. Instead, magic's primary affordance is to boost the morale of those involved in the ritual. In this respect, several supporters have noted that satire primarily 'preaches to the converted' (see Day, 2011, pp. 145–146; Gray, 2005, pp. 157–159; Quirk, 2015, p. 185).

If satire has political affordances, they mostly consist in harnessing emotional resources for political action among those who already agree with its message. As a case in point, the protest group behind Trump Baby only committed to flying their blimp during the President's 2019 visit to the UK on the condition of raising £30,000 for grassroots organisations that actively counteract his policies (Trumpbabyuk, 2019). Although they framed their balloon in 'a proud history of political satire in the UK' (Vickerstaff, 2019), they did not overstate the political impact of satire by itself.

Indeed, they explicitly acknowledged that '[t]hough demonstrably hilarious, flying a 20 ft high bright orange inflatable isn't going to change the world all on it's [*sic.*] own' (Trumpbabyuk, 2019). Instead, the real political affordance of Trump Baby is its contribution to sustaining 'a gathering of those who want to stand up to Trump's vile dialogue and politics' (Vickerstaff, 2019). The Trump Baby has become somewhat of a totem among a community of activists and protesters all over the world. Apart from the UK, Trump Baby blimps have appeared at protests in Ireland, France, Argentina and across the USA (Morgan, 2019).

The impact of Trump Baby on stimulating and sustaining political activism is not exceptional for satire. *Time* magazine even coined the 'John Oliver Effect' to acknowledge the satirist's impact on rallying support for political causes. Perhaps Oliver's most notable impact was the public response to his satire about plans by the American media regulator, FCC, to curtail net neutrality in 2014. After Oliver urged his viewers to protest, public response was so overwhelming that it crashed the FCC's website.

Tim Wu, who originally coined the phrase 'net neutrality', acknowledged that Oliver's efforts 'really made a difference' (CNN Staff, 2014). When the FCC ultimately passed new regulations that safeguarded net neutrality, research by the Berkman Klein Center for Internet & Society also confirmed that the YouTube video of Oliver's satirical exposé had been 'a prominent touch point for net neutrality advocates and the most popular link in the course of the controversy' (Faris, Roberts, Etling, Othman, & Benkler, 2015).

However, satire does not always lead to political success. After President Trump appointed a new chairman to the FCC, who opposed the previous regulation, Oliver once more rallied viewers to protest plans to abolish net neutrality. This time he even set up a specific domain (*GoFCCYourself.com*), which redirected to the FCC's proposal, to facilitate protest. Again, his request gathered significant public support, but this time, to no avail. At the end of 2017, the FCC introduced new regulation which effectively terminated net neutrality. This lack of success is reminiscent of the run-up to the 2016 election, when HBO sold over 50,000 hats with the slogan 'Make Donald Drumpf Again', which clearly did not swing the vote (Parker, 2016).

Satire may be able to stimulate political action, but it is by no means a guarantee for political success. However, political success is not the right standard to appreciate the political affordances of satire. Satirical practices such as *GoFCCYourself.com* or 'Make Donald Drumpf Again' may well have stimulated or sustained political action among Oliver's audience, even if that action ultimately did not translate into political success. In this respect, magic representations harness emotional resources towards achieving practical goals, but they do not 'magically' guarantee the achievement of those goals.

Concretely, although the New Zealand All Blacks perform a haka before every game, they are obviously not invincible. Yet, the point is that even when the All Blacks lose a game, it is not because the haka missed its emotional effect on the players. They may well have been as motivated and self-assured as usual, but still lost the game. Motivation and morale are necessary but seldom sufficient for winning a professional rugby game. Similarly, an emotional boost to sustain political action is typically essential for political success, but not always decisive.

As a magic representation, satire can have political affordances by motivating and sustaining political action, but it is no guarantee for political success. Hence, framing satire as magic is a challenge to overly heroic conceptions of satire's political impact. At the same time, satire's genuine political affordances should suffice to alleviate sceptical worries that *The Daily Show* or *Last Week Tonight* cannot inspire 'viewers to political activity' (Webber, 2013, p. 115) and 'will have little effect on political representation or political practice' (Webber, 2013, p. 113). Such scepticism is unwarranted, because the affordances of the genre to rally people around a political cause are clear, on both sides of the political spectrum.

There is not only a mass of anti-Trump satire, but the genre equally plays a significant role in pro-Trump online communities. Satirical memes are an important tool for an online community of Trump supporters to foster and sustain political action. In the aftermath of the 2016 election, online Trump supporters started identifying their co-ordinated social media efforts to sway public opinion as 'The Great Meme War' (Encyclopedia Dramatica Staff, 'The Great'). Many of these efforts were underpinned by a seemingly ridiculous, but cryptic notion of 'meme magic', that is, the idea that memes cause real-world results (Encyclopedia Dramatica Staff, 'Meme Magic').

Of course, such claims cannot be taken at face value, as they exhibit the ambiguity and dissimulation that characterises much internet humour. Nonetheless, John Gregoire (2017) is right when he links the professed 'magic' qualities of pro-Trump memes to their emotional impact on Trump supporters (pp. 4–25). At least for some social media users in online communities, like the subreddit r/The_Donald, satirical memes are a way of sustaining and promoting political action in support of Trump.

A particularly interesting example is the so-called 'NPC meme', which was popular in online communities like r/The Donald at the time of the 2018 US mid-term elections. NPC refers to Non-Playable Character, or a character in a video game which a player cannot select as an avatar (like the ghosts in Pac-Man). In a sense, NPCs have no human agency, because they are 'controlled' by the game's artificial intelligence. Over time, the idea of NPCs as units of consciousness without genuine human agency became applied to liberals and progressives in pro-Trump communities.

The visual representation of an NPC is a crudely drawn face with a blank stare, which either ironically endorses caricatural criticisms of Trump, including the groupthink slogan, 'Orange Man Bad' or ironically espouses progressive causes, such as critiquing 'privilege', 'patriarchy' and 'supremacy'. Around Halloween 2018, Redditors even posted photos of themselves in NPC Halloween costumes, ironically appropriating trademark leftie symbols, like Che Guevara T-shirts, and wearing NPC masks or bodysuits. Although the popularity of the NPC meme certainly frustrated some political opponents – one progressive website even called it 'dehumanization' (D'Anastasio, 2018) – its real political affordance lies in sustaining a communal sense of right-wing opposition to a perceived progressive hegemony, which underpins real political action.

Less than a week after Halloween, the 2018 mid-elections took place. Many Redditors on r/The Donald encouragingly shared messages about voting 'straight red', often disparaging NPCs in the process. The real political affordances of satire like the NPC meme are not to 'hurt' or 'cure' liberals, but exactly to harness emotional resources to sustain political action, like voting. The magic function of satirical memes to emotionally boost support for Trump should give those progressive critics who deny the political affordances of satire altogether, or who claim it only stimulates political apathy, some pause for thought. Satire may not seem like having much political impact, until its emotional qualities are successfully harnessed by political opponents.

JOURNALISM

Framed as a type of magic representation, satire clearly has real political affordances. Still, these should not be overstated. Moreover, satire's political affordances to emotionally stimulate political action (which may or may not result into political success) are not unique to the genre. There are other critical genres, especially journalistic genres like documentaries, which often have similar, and more pronounced, political affordances.

Consider the last episode of David Attenborough's *Blue Planet 2*, 'Our Blue Planet', which documented the harmful effects of plastic pollution on marine life. The episode showed harrowing images of sea birds who had died from consuming plastic waste, alongside dolphins who had been poisoned by microplastics. Much like Oliver in his satire on net neutrality, Attenborough concluded the episode with a call to action. Although Attenborough's appeal was not satirical, but deeply solemn, and the display of animal suffering shocking, rather than entertaining, its political affordances were comparable to Oliver's impact on the net neutrality debate.

In the wake of *Blue Planet 2*, UK media commented on the so-called 'Attenborough effect' (Guardian Staff, 2019). Theresa May, then Prime Minister, explicitly credited *Blue Planet 2*'s impact on public awareness when launching a new climate initiative (May, 2017) and later also gifted a box set to the Chinese President, Xi Jinping, to remind him of the damage of plastic waste (Elgot & Connett, 2018). Hence, *Blue Planet 2* had similar, if not even greater, political effects than *Last Week Tonight*. Satire's political affordances are, therefore, not unique. At the very least, they are comparable to the political affordances of journalistic genres – and the comparison between both genres is indeed common. In its first season, *Last Week Tonight* already received a Peabody Award for distinguished and meritorious public service by 'bringing satire and journalism even closer together' (2014).

This comparison with journalism certainly does not discredit the value of satire's political affordances, but it does make them less special and heroic. Although journalism is invaluable to the wellbeing of democracies, it is not by default heroic in a democratic context, where freedom of press and freedom of speech exist. There is nothing extraordinarily brave or courageous about a critical opinion piece in *The Guardian* or *The New York Times*, nor about Oliver's satirical dismissal of Donald Trump on *Last Week Tonight*. Pace Tucholsky (1919), the contemporary establishment (however defined) hardly dismisses such critique as intolerable 'crassness'.

At the same time, when satire is truly heroic, it is so for similar reasons as journalism. During the Arab Spring, the Morrocan rapper Mouad Belghouat, aka El Haked, was imprisoned for a satirical video clip about police corruption, which featured a policeman with a donkey's head (Freemuse Staff, 2011). Similarly, Egyptian satirist Bassem Youssef, who rose to international prominence as a guest on *The Daily Show with Jon Stewart*, ultimately had to flee the country for fear of his life (Youssef, 2017). The prosecution of El Haked and Youssef is similar to the imprisonment of more than 150 journalists under the authoritarian Erdogan regime (European Journalists Staff, 2019).

Satirists like Jon Stewart readily acknowledge that satire only really takes courage when it constitutes political opposition in non-democratic societies (RFE/RL Staff, 2009; Youssef 2017, cover endorsement). In such non-democratic contexts, satire is really a heroic act of opposition. Yet, it is not heroic simply because it is satire; it is heroic in the same way as all public opposition in this context, including critical journalism. If anything, satire's cloak of 'harmless' entertainment probably affords satirists more cover for their critique than journalists. According to Hu Yong, 'humor works as a natural form of encryption' in authoritarian contexts like China (cited in Larmer, 2011).

The cloak of entertainment may well provide satire with political affordances that are unavailable to other forms of critique, including journalism. For example, British satirist Josie Long argues that 'John Oliver is in a position where he has more people watching him than [political] commentators' (O'Hara, 2016). As entertainment, satire may indeed introduce some people to certain issues they would not seek out in journalistic contexts, and, as a magic representation, even motivate them to engage in political action. In this respect, when interviewing Oliver, fellow-satirist Stephen Colbert (2017) quipped, '[w]hat's the next thing you'll get me to care about that I didn't know I cared about?'

However, although there is indeed evidence that Oliver made some people care about net neutrality, who had not before, his impact should again not be overstated. Although Oliver's appeal to send objections to the FCC received a lot of media coverage and was responsible for a significant increase in online activity around the topic, research by the Berkman Klein Center established that, ultimately, 'the organized efforts by advocacy organizations to elicit comments was more successful' (Faris et al., 2015). Hence, even when satire's status as entertainment affords it to reach audiences who might otherwise not engage with political critique, there are more impactful forms of political action.

Satire does have genuine political affordances, but, at most, the genre is a steppingstone in support of more direct political action. Satirists typically have no problems to concede as much. When a reporter congratulated Oliver for bringing down the FCC's website, he responded, 'I didn't do anything. People did it. I merely pointed out the problem' (TMZ Staff, 2014). Pointing out a problem, and rallying people to resolve it, is certainly a valuable political affordance – but it does fall short of a heroic therapy for the socio-political ills of the world.

CONCLUSION

Satire has genuine political affordances. As a magic representation, satire can serve as an emotional booster to stimulate or sustain political action, as in the case of the Trump Baby blimp. However, such political action does not always entail political success. The idea of satire as a heroic therapy that cures socio-political sickness, therefore, introduces expectations that the genre cannot meet. Moreover, since the political impact of satire is only modest, especially compared to direct forms of political action, narrowly framing the genre's significance in terms of its political impact may ultimately make satire seem less significant than it really is. In the next chapter, I argue that satire's real significance should, therefore, not be framed as curing a sick world, but rather coping with it.

3

SATIRE AS THERAPY REVISITED: COPING WITH A SICK WORLD

INTRODUCTION

The previous chapter dismissed the heroic conception of satire as a cure for the socio-political ills of the world. Although the genre has real political affordances, they are modest. Nevertheless, 'therapy' is a fruitful concept to reassess the significance of satire beyond its political impact. Satirists regularly frame their satire as therapy for a world which is sick beyond full recovery. In this chapter, I identify the object of satire's therapy as the 'limits of critique'. Not only is the political impact of critique itself limited, so too are our resources in the service of critique.

These limits confront us with suffering that we cannot alleviate, and to which we may even be complicit. The limits of critique, therefore, reveal an existential conflict between moral care for others and prudent care of self. This conflict introduces mental health challenges (like neurotic perfectionism and depression) that satire seeks to address. Satire's therapeutic affordances have sometimes been framed in terms of 'catharsis', but I argue we need a better model to understand satire's significance as a resource for coping with a troubling socio-political environment.

THERAPY RECONSIDERED

Satirists are often the first to acknowledge their limited political impact. Instead, they commonly argue that satire really serves to address mental health challenges. According to Stephen Colbert, 'I have never had any illusion that what I am doing is changing the world' (Marchese, 2019). Instead, '[w]e're just trying to ease the pain of people who feel the world is going insane and no one is noticing' (Solomon, 2005). Similarly, satirical cartoonist Aaron McGruder explains that '[i]t's great to watch Colbert and (...) it keeps you sane' (Cavna, 2008).

According to critics and fans, satire like *The Daily Show with Jon Stewart* is an 'oasis of sanity' (Taylor, 2004), 'a touchstone of sanity' (Boler & Thurpin, 2008, p. 397) and 'a strain of sanity in a world that seemed increasingly scary, dangerous, and irrational' (Cuddeback, 2015). For this reason, Jacob Sugerman (2016) identifies Stewart as 'equal parts news anchor and therapist for liberals of a certain persuasion'. Others similarly describe *Saturday Night Live*'s satire of Donald Trump as 'an escape from their distress through satire' which functions as 'a coping mechanism' because it offers 'a brief but necessary reprieve from the reality of Trump's presidency' (Hi's Eye Staff, 2017).

Smaller satire publications also regularly present themselves as a 'political sanity medicine' against 'depressing' politics and try to attract audiences with slogans like 'Rescue Your Sanity in the Age of Trump' (Humor Times Staff, n.d.). Others heroically declare to take 'on the thankless and oft overlooked role of defending the public's sanity by making people laugh' (Smug Staff, 2019). Similarly, the idea that satire preserves 'sanity' is popular among bloggers (Khan, 2018; Vankadara, 2017). Occasionally, mental health issues, such as 'depression', are explicitly listed as what drives satirists, like the Iranian comedian Kambiz Hosseini (Nehring, 2013).

Mental ill health among comedians has received significant critical attention (see Dessau, 2012). Performances of stand-up comedians like Hannah Gadsby, Ruby Wax and Felicity Ward have also addressed experiences of mental illness. As a result, high-profile cases such as Robin Williams's suicide have sometimes fuelled speculation about whether 'Genius and Depression [come] from the Same Well?' (Shedler, 2014). These speculations are highly debatable (Lintott, 2020). Therefore, I make no claims that the creativity of satirists follows from mental ill health, nor that satirists (or their audiences) are especially predisposed or prone to mental health issues.

Satire should also be distinguished from comedy (see Chapter 1). Whereas comedy broadly has the purpose to amuse, satire not only sets out to entertain, but also to critique. Unlike comedy, satire, therefore, always reacts against a word which is itself 'insane', and which risks compromising our mental health, unless we find a way to cope with it. The South African satirist, John Curtis, argues that 'as the world spirals into more craziness, cartoonists have constantly stepped up to the plate and met the challenges head on' (cited in Jenkin, 2017). Similarly, in *The Madhouse Effect*, climate change specialist

Michael E. Mann and cartoonist Tom Toles (2016, p. 10) frame their satire as a way 'to escape the madhouse'.

In the eye of the satirist, the world is sick beyond full recovery. As the Egyptian satirist Bassem Youssef (2017) puts it, 'I can firmly state that in all the possible outcomes for our universe, the one remaining constant is that the Arab world will always be fucked' (p. 281). Hence, according to Youssef (2017), '[t]here is too much infatuation with the idea that satire can make a difference' (p. 181). The point is not that satire promotes political apathy or is inadequate as critique. Rather, even the most sustained political action is unlikely to redress all social injustice. Critique has its limits – and satire helps us to cope with that.

THE LIMITS OF CRITIQUE

Satirists often acknowledge the limits of critique. Take Margaret Atwood's *The Handmaid's Tale* and *South Park*'s 'The Hobbit', which both satirise how patriarchy impacts the wellbeing of women. Despite a commitment to critique, their respective endings also imply that critique fails to fully redress patriarchal injustice. These endings should not be mistaken for pessimism or apathy, which dismisses all critique as futile. Instead, serious commitment to critique also entails accepting its limits. Therefore, instead of being pessimistic, these endings are realistic.

The Handmaid's Tale satirises the rise of the religious right during Ronald Reagan's presidency. At the time, Atwood described her satire as 'play[ing] with hypotheses', specifically

> *some of the statements that are being made by the 'Evangelical fundamentalist right.' If a woman's place is in the home, then what? If you actually decide to enforce that, what follows? (Rothstein, 1986)*

As a satirical thought experiment, Atwood develops a predictive fantasy about the nearby future, in which a group of puritan hardliners has overthrown the US parliament and instituted a patriarchal theocracy (called Gilead).

In this theocracy, a class of fertile women (the 'handmaids') serve as concubines and surrogate mothers to a ruling class of commanders, whose wives have become infertile due to environmental pollution and STD epidemics. Once a month, every handmaid must endure ritualized rape by her commander, alongside his wife, until she bears him a child – an act of simultaneous polygamy justified by Biblical principles.

The story unfolds from the first-person perspective of one handmaid, Offred (a patronymic), who relates her experiences before and during the Gilead regime. Her story ends ambiguously, as she is taken away in the back of a van by either the secret police (who have come to arrest her) or members of an underground network (who will escort her to safety abroad). The novel's epilogue is not told from Offred's perspective but features a 'partial transcript of the proceedings of the Twelfth Symposium on Gileadean Studies' (Atwood, 1996 [1985], p. 331).

Atwood ultimately frames the eponymous handmaid's tale as presented by two editors, who stumbled on recordings of it in 2195. She was inspired by the appendix on the principles of newspeak in George Orwell's *1984*, which is 'written in standard English, in the third person, and in the past tense, which can only mean that the regime has fallen, and that language and individuality have survived' (Atwood, 2003). Similarly, by including the partial proceedings to an academic conference at the end of *The Handmaid's Tale*, Atwood signals that the 'Gilead Period' ultimately passed.

Fortunately, matters have clearly improved after the fall of Gilead. The scheduled fishing trip and nature excursion during the symposium reveal that the climate and environment have at least partly recovered. Moreover, Professor Maryann Crescent Moon's function as conference chair indicates that women can again pursue professional careers. Nevertheless, Atwood's optimism is tempered by wry irony. Professor Pieixoto, who co-edited Offred's diary, delivers a keynote address that frequently indulges in sexist remarks, much to the delight of his audience. Hence, despite improvement after the fall of Gilead, women still face sexist discrimination at the end of *The Handmaid's Tale*.

The restraint of Atwood's optimism is not unwarranted, especially as people once more turned to her cautionary satire 'for guidance and insight' in the era of Trump and the *Access Hollywood* tape scandal (Alter, 2017). Around that time, Hulu also released the first season of a new adaptation, which critics framed as a timely 'warning, about how oppression can creep up on you, and what happens when women's lives are no longer their own' (Nicholson, 2017). Clearly, the enduring relevance of *The Handmaid's Tale* is a testimony to Atwood's caution about the political impact of her critique.

A similar caution characterises *South Park*'s 'The Hobbit' (Parker & Stone, 2013), which fans praised as 'the series' most biting social satire of the whole [seventeenth] season' (Crow, 2013). 'The Hobbit' satirises the impact of photoshopped female bodies on the self-esteem and wellbeing of young girls and women. In the episode, 9-year old cheerleader Lisa Berger struggles with her body image. Lisa is lethargic because, as she tells her teammates, '[e]very cheerleading squad has "the fat ugly cheerleader" and that's me.' In response, the squad captain, Wendy Testaburger, retorts that Lisa simply suffers from 'a bad self-image' and should go on a date, which would do 'wonders for [her] confidence'.

However, when Lisa asks somebody out, Butters Stotch obliviously responds, 'I appreciate the offer, but you're too fat for me'. Later, Wendy angrily confronts Butters and tells him that Lisa is 'a little overweight, but that's pretty normal for a girl in the fourth grade!' He steadfastly responds, 'Kim Kardashian is skinny and she just had a baby!' Butters continues,

> *I have a different standard when it comes to my women. I want a woman who takes care of herself and knows how to look good, who's got perfect skin and no splotches on her legs, and perfect everything.*

As the satirical target of the episode appears in full focus, a baffled Wendy responds,

> *This is a fantasy, you moron! Have you ever heard of Photoshop?! Kim Kardashian is a short, overweight woman who manipulates her image and makes average girls feel horrible about themselves! Look it up, stupid! In real life, Kim Kardashian has the body of a hobbit!*

Afterwards, Butters complains to the school councillor, Mr Mackey, who surprisingly reprimands Wendy for having 'called Butters' girlfriend a hobbit.' Mr Mackey also dismisses Wendy's defence that she is 'the biggest feminist in this school' and ignorantly brands her 'a hater' who is 'jelly' of Kim Kardashian's success.

Through an intricate web of analogies, *South Park*'s 'The Hobbit' satirises the impact of photoshopped bodies on girls and women, like Lisa. The episode alludes to Kim Kardashian's appearance in a music video of her then-fiancé Kayne West, with her post-pregnancy weight airbrushed out in postproduction. The naïve Butters is a stand-in for unreflective heterosexual boys and men who are fooled by the standards of female beauty imposed by photoshopped imagery. Similarly, the incompetent school councillor, Mr Mackey, represents authorities who have failed to adequately respond to the issue. Finally, Wendy's predicament, as voice of progressive reason in *South Park*, is analogous to feminists whose critique is perversely dismissed as sexual jealousy.

For the rest of the episode, Wendy is on a mission to end the social injustice of photoshopped female bodies. She first shows Butters how easy it is to make

Lisa look 'hot' by using Photoshop. However, mistaking the manipulated image for the real Lisa, Butters now desperately wants to date her. Yet, by that time, the photoshopped picture went viral, and Lisa is already dating another, more popular boy, Clyde (who, ironically, was among a group of boys that originally mocked Butters for getting 'asked out by a fat girl'). Now, Clyde gleefully strides across the school, showing everyone Lisa's photoshopped image on his phone, while holding the real Lisa by the arm.

The situation is absurd, but the absurdity is only clear to Wendy. Lisa soon becomes the most popular girl in the school and the other cheerleaders ask Wendy to 'do for us what you did for Lisa and help with our imperfections'. When Wendy refuses, the other girls find help elsewhere to photoshop their social media pictures. In turn, Wendy's boyfriend asks her for a photoshopped image that removes 'any imperfections'. She refuses, once more. By now, Wendy is completely ostracised from the school community and has become as lethargic as Lisa at the beginning of the episode.

However, Wendy does not abandon her critical mission and takes her grievances to national television. She argues that '[w]atching what Photoshop is doing to society ... Little girls are aspiring to have bodies they can't possibly have! We have to put a stop to it'. Again, Wendy's feminist critique is dismissed as sexual jealousy, as the talk show host dismisses her for 'being jelly' and 'being a hater'. In response, Wendy swears, 'I'm not going to rest until photoshopped images are required to be labelled for what they are! Fake! And nothing in this world is going to stop me!'

Yet, the ending of the episode ironically undercuts Wendy's heartfelt determination. In the next scene, Kayne West surprises Wendy in her sleep, and emotionally blackmails her to silence her critique, for the sake of his fiancée's career. Exasperated, Wendy finally breaks. The episode concludes as she photoshops her picture and e-mails it to everybody in the school, tears rolling from her eyes. Wendy's critique ultimately amounts to nothing as self-preservation forces her to join a movement she cannot beat.

South Park's 'The Hobbit' is ambiguous about the impact of critique. Stephen Groening (2008) argues that the 'ironic satire of *South Park*' is a 'cynical irony: calling attention to injustices and proposing that nothing can be done' (p. 120). Matthew Becker (2008) similarly claims that 'the political worldview of *South Park* is (...) characterized by irony, apathy, feelings of disenfranchisement, and deep cynicism' (p. 147). The same accusations have been levelled at the satire of *The Simpsons*, which, according to Carl Matheson (2001), cultivates a 'hyper-irony' and 'does not promote anything, because its humor works by putting forward positions only in order to undercut them' (p. 118).

These scholars are concerned that satire like *South Park* and *The Simpsons* promotes a wryly ironic worldview, according to which contemporary culture is sick beyond recovery, but one can remain happy by 'living at a somewhat oblique angle to that culture' (Dettmar, 2004, p. 88). Simon Critchley (1997) identifies such a worldview as a conformist nihilism – '*don't worry, be happy*' (p. 11, original emphasis). Similarly, James Wallace (2001) argues that satire like *The Simpsons* 'is at once nihilistic (everything is a target) and conservative (the traditional social order endures)' (p. 147).

Such conformist nihilism is associated with postmodernity, which, according to Peter Sloterdijk (1987), is permeated by 'a universal, diffuse cynicism' (p. 3). Duncan Beard (2004) argues that postmodern satire 'does not conform to earlier definitions of satire, which maintain that satirical criticism must be based upon an implicit or explicit set of values' and, therefore, 'rarely finds a positive voice of rejuvenation to provide alternative visions for situations that have been satirically criticized as unfavorable' (p. 287). Carl Bybee and Ashley Overbeck (2001), therefore, criticise *The Simpsons* for formulating 'a postmodernism of despair', since 'all social or political action is equally futile and absurd' (p. 10).

Sloterdijk (1987, p.5) defines cynicism as 'enlightened false consciousness' which involves

> *a radical, ironic treatment* (Ironisierung) *of ethics and of social conventions, as if universal laws existed only for the stupid, while that fatally clever smile plays on the lips of those in the know. (p. 4)*

Enlightened consciousness is the desired outcome of critique, which targets fundamentally naïve false consciousness. Those who do wrong are unaware they are doing it; critique, therefore, serves to expose the wrongness and make naïve false consciousness enlightened (Žižek, 1989, p. 28).

Of course, this ideal of critique is itself naïve. As 'The Hobbit' demonstrates, sometimes critique fails to get through to naïve targets like Butters or Mr Mackey. Moreover, when Kanye West confronts Wendy, he already knows about the 'magic power, called Photoshop' which made 'the little hobbit (...) beautiful'. West also admits that

> *even though she still couldn't sing like Beyoncé, or dance like Beyoncé, or act like Beyoncé, or be a decent human being like Beyoncé, the little hobbit was looked up to and loved, just like Beyoncé!*

He knows about the falsehood, but he does not 'care' – and neither did the real Kim Kardashian, who 'broke the internet' about a year later with a nude and obviously photoshopped cover for *Paper* magazine.

Hardened perpetrators of social injustice are unlikely to be disturbed by critique because they are not driven by a desire for truth, but a will for power (Sloterdijk, 1987, p. xxvii/3). These are the real cynics, because '*they know* it, but *they are doing* it anyway' (Žižek, 1989, p. 28, original emphasis). Such cynicism is prominent in the contemporary context of post-truth politics, where a power-hungry political elite continually flouts the basic virtues of truth. In response, some argue that critique has itself become cynical, including so-called postmodern satire, because it suggests that nothing can be done about the falsehoods it reveals (Groening, 2008, p. 114–116).

However, I disagree that the ending of 'The Hobbit' or *The Handmaid's Tale* promotes cynicism. For one, both stories make us empathise with the plight of their protagonists. There is no sense of smug and comfortable knowingness when Offred is taken in the back of the van, nor when tears role down Wendy's face. These are heartfelt, not cynical, moments. Moreover, how realistic would it have been if Wendy simply resolved the harmful representation of photoshopped female bodes by the end of the episode? Similarly, history has proven Margaret Atwood right to be cautious about the advance of women's rights.

Such so-called postmodern satire is not so different from what came before. Classic satires, like Swift's *Gulliver's Travels*, similarly reflected on 'the satirist's role' which involves dealing with 'the knowledge that he has had all along: that people are as they are, and satire never seems to reform them' (Roberts, 2001, p. xvii). Moreover, when classic satires like Swift's (1729) *A Modest Proposal* do outline reforms, it is often with an ironic sense of exasperation that 'no man talk to me of these and the like expedients' – and little hope that someone actually will.

Satire also need not explicitly outline reforms to emotionally sustain or boost political action. As discussed, the Trump Baby blimp does nothing more than ridicule the professed childish behaviour of the US President, but it still sustains support for grassroots organisations that oppose his policies. Moreover, the ambiguity of *South Park*'s ending does not necessarily cancel the emotional impact of what came before, nor does it aim to do so. If anything, Wendy's heartfelt sadness has the power to sting *South Park*'s audience into political reflection, if not action.

In this respect, the most stinging critique in 'The Hobbit' is a montage of the cheerleaders in the gym, working out 'to trim that fat and tone those bodies' – not through physical exercise, but through Photoshop. The montage shows how Nicole, a black cheerleader, whitewashes her picture by toning down her skin and straightening her curly hair. Similarly, Timmy, a boy in a motorised wheelchair, is stripped of his mental and physical handicaps as if they were aesthetic imperfections. *South Park* succinctly captures the malice of photoshopped imagery by showing how it perpetuates racist and ableist standards of beauty. The sting of this critique is hardly undone by Wendy's inability to change the situation.

Therefore, the ending of 'The Hobbit' is ultimately not cynical but realistic about critique's prospects. Although sustained political action has now resulted in some backlash against photoshopped bodies on social media, it gives to wonder whether trends like 'no make-up' or 'just-woke-up' selfies really are free from manipulation in pre- or post-production. Moreover, these trends may well perpetuate unrealistic beauty standards in other ways. Similarly, although advertisements have started to showcase greater diversity in body types, there is still a long way to go. Instead of promoting cynicism, 'The Hobbit' really deals with the emotional strain on Wendy's wellbeing as she confronts the limits of her political action and her personal resources for critique.

TRUTH AND MENTAL ILLNESS

South Park's 'The Hobbit' and Atwood's *The Handmaid's Tale* confront a difficult truth about the limits of critique. The centrality of truth to satire is often associated with the heroic conception of the genre as a therapy for the ills of the world. Satire's professed mission to speak 'truth to power' should be taken with a pinch of salt, given its common status as fiction (Declercq, 2019) and its tendency for simplification and exaggeration (Declercq, 2018b). Nevertheless, satirists who are truly serious about critique must uphold what Bernard Williams (2002) calls '[t]he value of truthfulness [which] embraces the need to find out the truth, to hold on to it, and to tell it – in particular, to oneself' (p. 13).

Satirical cartoonist Dan Perkins (2014a), aka Tom Tomorrow, states that his 'concerns are: is it funny? and is it true? And sometimes you can even fudge it on funny, as long as it's true enough to matter'. He specifically refers to '[t]he intensity of the vitriol and the hate mail' during 'the years after 9/11', which 'were tough times to be a political satirist' (Perkins, 2014b). He clarifies that

> *[t]here's a reason many of today's prominent liberal voices either supported the wars or just kept quiet. In a way I wish I'd had the option, but I had a weekly deadline to meet and a nagging compulsion to speak the truth as I saw it. (Perkins, 2014b)*

Despite heroic overtones, Perkins is right that committed satirists are driven by a moral compulsion to find out the truth and share it with others, even if their truthfulness is unsettling. Just think of Wendy, who was ostracised for her critique of photoshopped female bodies. Drawing on Nietzsche, Williams (2002) specifies that such commitment to truthfulness rests in a moral conviction, rather than a calculus of utility (p. 14). Devotion to critique ultimately means facing its limits – which often comes at a price for our wellbeing, as is clear from Wendy's plight.

Nietzsche's (2001 [1888]) challenge is how we cope with truth in a post-metaphysical world where 'God is dead!' (p. 120). According to Williams (2002),

> *[o]ne of Nietzsche's most striking qualities is the obstinacy with which he held to an ideal of truthfulness that would not allow us to falsify or forget the horrors of the world (...) [especially after he revealed that] the traditional metaphysical conceptions which have helped us to make sense of the world, and in particular to bear its horrors, have been terminally broken down. (p. 13)*

In a post-metaphysical world, '[n]one of us honestly retain the consolations of religion or teleology – that it is the fault of the poor, or that they will get their reward later' (Blackburn, 1986, p. 202).

Nietzsche's response to this challenge has often been framed as a soggy relativism, according to which there are no truths – and, hence, 'anything goes'. However, according to Williams (2001, p. xx; 2002, p. 13), 'so far from his seeing truth as dispensable or malleable, [Nietzsche's] main question is how it can be made bearable'. After Nietzsche, '[t]he hope can no longer be that the truth, enough truth, the whole truth, will set us free' (Williams, 2002, p. 268). This problem constitutes the limits of critique. Satirists who are committed to critique set out to reveal the truth about social injustice, but they equally must face the truth that the political impact of critique is limited.

Consider 'a generic Tom Tomorrow cartoon, applicable to any breaking news story that may occur during Tom's current vacation' (Perkins 2016, p. 401). In the cartoon, Sparky the Wonder Penguin, Perkins's exasperated stand-in, faces a recurring target, Biff, whose naïve perspective is abstracted to 'misguided enthusiasm for social trend or political event based on uncritical acceptance of superficial mainstream news coverage'. Sparky initially responds with similarly abstract 'castigation of misguided enthusiasm' and presents 'a more cynical view of the probable though unstated motives of the politicians or other protagonists involved!' However, Sparky ultimately resigns himself to 'acknowledging that alternative analysis is unlikely to gain widespread acceptance'.

The punchline of Perkins's cartoon is that his satire 'always stays on top of the news, even when it doesn't!' Much like the ironic endings of *The Handmaid's Tale* and 'The Hobbit', Perkins's punchline serves to wryly acknowledge the limits of critique. It is not for want of trying – and Sparky will try again in next week's cartoon – but reflexive satirists cannot hope that truth will fully dispel injustice. The point is not that satire and critique never have political impact. It is just that sometimes (perhaps even often), despite committed political action, things just do not get any better.

The limits of critique may seem like reason to devote ourselves unabatedly to improving the world. However, satirists typically also acknowledge the limits of their own resources to sustain critique. In 'The Hobbit', Wendy pursues her mission with unabated zeal; whenever we see her, she is exposing the harmfulness of photoshopped female bodies, but to no avail. In the end, she cracks and joins the trend she so zealously opposed. And at that stage, who could really blame her? She pushed her critique to the point of compromising her own wellbeing.

Although Simon Blackburn (2003) urges that 'we should do our best with the [problems] we can solve' (p. 43), he also concedes that '[w]e simply cannot shoulder the burden of the entire world' (Blackburn, 1998, p. 221). Instead, '[w]e need and cherish spheres within which we are completely absorbed by private concern and emotion' (Blackburn, 1998, p. 22). Therefore, Blackburn (2003) advises that 'the right reaction is to look for moral principles that are not impractical, and not limitless in their demands' (p. 43), nor should our care for others become 'obsessive and neurotic' (Blackburn, 1998, p. 16).

The limitless care for others constitutes neurotic perfectionism (see Declercq, 2020). A neurotic perfectionist 'compare[s] their values with inaccessible goals' (Geranmayepoura & Besharata, 2010, p. 634). Therefore,

> *[n]o matter how much [neurotic perfectionists] have accomplished, they always feel that they could have done – and should have done – better, and thus respond with shame and guilt regarding their alleged underachievements. (Stoeber, Harris, & Moon, 2007, p. 131)*

Moral perfectionists, specifically, can be 'destroyed by neurotic and obsessive misplaced guilt [and shame] (…) and the feeling of having let themselves or others down, when no such feelings are appropriate' (Blackburn, 1998, p. 16).

The risk of neurotic perfectionism explains why satirists are wise to acknowledge the limits of critique. Reflexive satirists are not cynics, but realists who deal with their own imperfection. Otherwise, they risk becoming consumed by the failure to meet unattainable goals. Although the world's problems stipulate a moral care for others, we would recklessly compromise our mental health if that care were unabated. Reflexive satirists turn to satire to negotiate this 'uncomfortable' tension between care for others and care of self (Blackburn, 1998, p. 232).

This existential tension introduces mental health challenges, which are insightfully developed through the satirical representation of Chidi Anagonye in the comedy series, *The Good Place*. Chidi is a deceased ethics professor, who thinks he is now in the eponymous 'good place'; as opposed to most humans, who ultimately end up in the 'bad place'. Entry to a blissful afterlife is governed by a strict point system. Every human action is awarded positive or negative points, based on its moral goodness. At death, an individual's points are tallied up and only the highest final scores secure entry into the 'good place'.

Chidi is a moral perfectionist, who, during his life, always aspired to the perfect moral choice. He is unlike most people, who fail to make it into the 'good place' because (as he himself puts it) they 'think that they're making one choice, but they're actually making dozens of choices they don't even know they're making' (Schur, 2019a). Yet, Chidi's tragic flaw is exactly his painful awareness of all the consequences of his decisions. As a result, Chidi's moral deliberation is so neurotic and obsessive that it becomes completely unsuccessful and he never reaches a decision (or incessantly postpones).

Ultimately, Chidi realises that he is really in an experimental version of the 'bad place', where 'sinners' experience a level of psychological torture equivalent to their character flaws. At first, he is incredulous, but then guiltily admits to using 'almond milk in my coffee, even though I knew about the negative environmental impact!' (Schur, 2017). Of course, Chidi quickly realises that his real sin was not his imperfect environmentalism, but his constant indecisiveness, which was a torture for everyone in his environment, including himself. Therefore, what really makes the 'bad place' so bad is that Chidi must constantly make decisions, which makes his stomach hurt.

Yet, the guilt that Chidi feels about using almond milk is important, because it is an effort to offset the environmental impact of dairy which itself falls short of the moral mark. According to *The Good Place*, modern life has complicated even benign acts of altruism, like buying birthday presents:

> *In 1534, Douglass Wynegar of Hawkhurst, England, gave his grandmother roses for her birthday. He picked them himself, walked them over to her, she was happy … boom, 145 points. (…) In 2009, Doug Ewing of Scaggsville, Maryland, also gave his grandmother a dozen roses, but he lost four points. Why? Because he ordered roses using a cell phone that was made in a sweatshop. The flowers were grown with toxic pesticides, picked by exploited migrant workers, delivered from thousands of miles away, which created a massive carbon footprint, and his money went to a billionaire racist CEO who sends his female employees pictures of his genitals. (Schur, 2019b)*

The message is clear: 'Life now is so complicated, it's impossible for anyone to be good enough for the "good place"' (Schur, 2019a).

Due to the rise of globalised information technology, we are now, more than ever, aware of the consequences of our actions. Like Nietzsche, we must accept that

> *a sense of the world's achievements and glories (...) cannot in common honesty be separated from the knowledge of the horrors that have been involved in bringing these things about. (Williams, 2002, p. xiv)*

Nietzsche's challenge is, therefore, to live with the knowledge that suffering exists which we cannot alleviate, and to which we may even be complicit.

According to Williams, Nietzsche (2001) had 'a hyper-sensitivity to suffering' (p. xiv) and, therefore, grasped that 'anyone who really understood and held in his mind the horrors of the world would be crushed or choked by them' (p. xv). However, if we devoted our lives unabatedly to critique, to terminate the world's horrors and suffering, we would become neurotic perfectionists like Chidi, psychologically tormented by our inability to live up to inaccessible goals. To preserve our own wellbeing, we must, therefore, face insoluble suffering (to which we may even be complicit). Yet, doing so introduces mental health challenges of its own.

The overload of bad news in an age of globalised information technology can stimulate 'political burnout' (Pierquet, 2018) and 'political depression' (Cvetkovich, 2012, p. 1). For example, prolonged uncertainty about the impact of the UK's exit from the European Union has generated so-called 'Brexit anxiety' (Weaver, 2018). One NGO in London even offered free counselling to counter the psychological distress caused by worrying over Brexit (EA Staff). A similar kind of mental health challenge is an 'ecologically induced dread' (Albrecht, 2011, p. 49) or what Per Espen Stoknes (2015) calls the 'Mordor of eco-anxiety, despair and, depression'.

Sceptics warn that concepts like 'Brexit anxiety' and the general medicalisation of legitimate feelings of anger and pain may weaken the political agency of individuals (Degerman, 2019). Others similarly argue that '[e]co-anxiety is not an illness but a perfectly rational response to the enormity of our problems' (Lawton, 2019), or that experiences of mental ill health actually offer unique avenues for political action. Specifically, Ann Cvetkovich (2012) argues that political depression has valuable political affordances (p. 111), while Stoknes (2015) proposes that climate grief reconnects us with the planet (pp. 170–189).

Granted, negative emotions motivate political action; if we are not angry or upset about injustice, we are unlikely to do anything about it. Nonetheless, excessive emotional turmoil can turn pathological and become detrimental to our mental health. Our challenge is, therefore, to fend off depressive and anxious feelings by striking a balance between caring for others, without succumbing to neurotic perfectionism, and caring for ourselves, without succumbing to apathy or cynicism. As Valerie Tiberius (2008) puts it, we simply must learn to 'live with the conflict' (p. 179) and find a 'strategy for coping with an imperfect world' (p. 180).

Satirists often present their satire as a therapy for a world that is sick beyond full recovery. For example, Perkins (1993) frames his satire 'as a defense mechanism' and explains 'I have learned to channel my anger through it, and I hope that to some extent it serves this purpose for my readers as well' (p. 209). He further explains how

> *sometimes a reader will write to say that a cartoon on a given topic is 'depressingly accurate,' or that they would laugh if they weren't too busy crying. (...) But I hope they laugh anyway. Cause that's the whole point of this job. It's a two-pronged assault. There are lot[s] of things in this world you need to be outraged about, but outrage unchecked by laughter will eat you up inside. You need to laugh. That's where we come in. (Perkins 2013)*

If Perkins is right, satire helps to sustain good mental health by negotiating a balance between the demands of critique and its limits.

SISYPHUS LABOUR

The job of the satirist is usefully framed as a Sisyphus labour. In Greek mythology, the Corinthian king Sisyphus was condemned by the gods to roll a heavy rock to the top of a mountain for all eternity, only for it to roll back each time. Similarly, Perkins argues that

> *[y]ou have to want to save the world in order to get up every day and do this work [satire], but in order to maintain your sanity, you simultaneously have to understand that you're just not going to. (Rall, 2002, p. 28)*

In *The Myth of Sisyphus*, Albert Camus (1955) adopts the image of a Sisyphus labour as a metaphor for the absurdity of life. According to Camus (1955), the feeling of absurdity arises because 'in a universe suddenly divested of illusions and lights, man feels an alien, a stranger' (p. 5). Absurdity is a feeling which arises from the unbridgeable divide between our spiritual desire for existential meaning and the universe's cold indifference in a post-metaphysical world (Camus, 1955, p. 15).

This feeling of absurdity can stimulate depression, which is a mood disorder (Godderis, 2000, p. 173). Jan Godderis (2000) refers to a German synonym for 'mood', *Stimmung*, with its musical connotations of 'tuning' (into something), to classify depression as a disorder whereby an individual is 'out of tune' with their environment (pp. 175–176). This asynchrony manifests itself primarily as a disturbance of the circadian rhythm, which regulates the sleep pattern (Godderis, 2000, pp. 176–177). Similarly, Camus (1955) describes absurdity as the 'incalculable feeling that deprives the mind of the sleep necessary to life' (p. 5).

For Camus (1955), Sisyphus is a hero because he has accepted the absurdity of life without 'hope' (p. 7) and without succumbing to 'a metaphysic of consolation' (p. 34). He knows that his efforts are pointless, but he revolts against this pointlessness by passionately engaging in those efforts anyway – even if they do not make a difference (Camus, 1955, p. 83). Similarly, Glenn Dixon (2008) describes Perkins's satire as 'the outcry of an exasperated, angry, even baffled voice in times that are absurd beyond imagining', while Glenn Greenwald (2006) argues that his cartoons convey how 'our political dialogue has degenerated well into the realm of the absurd'.

Nonetheless, there is a significant difference between reflexive satirists and absurdist heroes. According to Camus (1955), '[o]ne must imagine Sisyphus happy' (p. 123). He is a happy nihilist who acts beyond good and evil. As Camus (1955) puts it, '[b]elief in the meaning of life always implies a scale of values, a choice, our preferences. Belief in the absurd, according to our definitions, teaches the contrary' (Camus, 1955, p. 45). The absurdist hero meets the challenge of the absurd by accepting his fate without hope for change; everything that happens is of equal value, that is, no value at all. Sisyphus revolts against lethargy by living life to the fullest in the present, without concern for the value of his actions (Camus, 1955, p. 45).

However, reflexive satirists do not exhibit an 'absurd joy' (Camus, 1955, p. 93). Instead, satirical cartoonist Jen Sorensen (2014) describes her job as 'worrying about how humanity is destroying itself'. Whatever enjoyment satire provides, it seems to serve as therapy for absurdity – not a celebration. Therefore, Sorensen (2008) explains that '[m]any cartoons [of mine] are not overtly political. One can only write so many strips about torture before one needs to lighten up with a riff on Gucci flipflops' (p. 7).

Moreover, Camus specifies that 'an absurd attitude, if it is to remain so, must remain aware of its gratuitousness. So it is with the work of art' (Camus, 1955, p. 102). In other words, artists must give up all hope that their efforts will achieve anything, for if the work 'sacrifices to illusions and arouses hope, it ceases to be gratuitous' (Camus, 1955, p, 102). However, although satirists often acknowledge the limits of critique, absurd gratuitousness is usually alien to their creative practice.

For example, although Perkins acknowledges that his 'little weekly cartoon' is 'not going to change the world', he nonetheless 'think[s] it's useful to point out absurdities' (Elias, 2003). Further, he argues that

> *I wouldn't do what I do if there wasn't an inherent optimism there. It's an optimism tinged with bitterness and frustration but if I didn't believe that things can get better then I would go live in some remote farmhouse somewhere and ignore the world entirely. (Hansen, 2003)*

Similarly, satirical cartoonist Ted Rall (2002) quips, '[c]artooning won't change the world, but that's no reason not to try' (p. 7). According to Rall (2002), 'I don't think cartooning can change the world, but you need the illusion that it could to produce earnest, meaningful work' (pp. 120–121). For this reason, Michael Charrington (2001) refers to Rall as 'a hopeless optimist; he's optimistic while entertaining no hope' (p. 6).

Matt Bors (2013) displays a similar hopeless optimism. He wryly jokes,

> *I hope that a few of my cartoons will be unearthed from the ruins of our forthcoming apocalypse as proof that we weren't all on board with the way things were going. (p. v)*

Bors (2013) captures the Sisyphean nature of satire by claiming

> *[s]ometimes the only thing you can do is mark up public surfaces and get everyone to laugh at the people running things. It's a small form of resistance, a minor annoyance at best to those in power. But if they insist on doing us this way, I'm at least going to make them come out every morning and repaint the damn walls. (p. vi)*

According to Bors,

> *I don't* like *the fact that the world is run by a revolving cast of douche bags, but I do like cartooning about it! I like addressing reality, the way things are, without sugar coating them. Satire is a way to stay sane amid all this. (Arrant, 2012, original emphasis)*

As opposed to Camus's Sisyphus, reflexive satirists do revolt against political absurdities, even if they know the impact of their critique to be limited. Yet, to cope with the absurdity of their situation, they often frame the limits of critique with a wry sense of irony. This strategy seems to introduce some psychological distance to sustain good mental health – both for themselves and their audiences. As Ben Bagdikian argues, '[t]he current political scene creates two impulses, to jump off a bridge or to laugh. Luckily, Tom Tomorrow [aka Dan Perkins] gives us a chance to laugh' (Perkins, n.d.). Hence, there is an intuitive consensus that satire serves as a therapy for satirists and audiences in a depressing socio-political environment. But how does it have these therapeutic qualities?

THE LIMITS OF CATHARSIS

The therapeutic affordances of satire have often been framed in terms of 'catharsis'. According to Jon Stewart, 'if [satire]'s purpose was social change, we're not picking a very effective avenue' (Fettis, 2015). Stewart argues that 'the real outcome of satire is typically catharsis' (Fettis, 2015) and likens the emotional impact of satire to 'a release valve' (RFE/RL Staff, 2009). Similarly, the production team of *Full Frontal with Samantha Bee* regularly refers to the show as 'a wonderful 21-minute catharsis' (Mulkerrins, 2018) and something done 'for our own catharsis' (Procassini, 2017).

The idea that satire has a cathartic function which releases or 'vents' emotional tension was already common among Roman satirists like Juvenal and Persius (Keane, 2015, p. 38; Sutherland, 1958, p. 4). Modern theories of satirical catharsis similarly frame satiric purgation as the expulsion of otherwise distressing feelings and emotions (Kivistö, 2009, p. 52). Alice Birney (1973) considers satire a 'safety-valve' that purges audiences of the impulse to censure society and improve the world (p. 147). According to Birney (1973), '[t]he inhibition of satiric catharsis in a play prevents the audience's aesthetic inebriation and results in a state of anxiety, an aggravated awareness of social ill' (p. 148).

The catharsis model (or safety valve model) captures the intuition that satire affords relief from a troubling socio-political environment (see Gini, 2017, p. xxiii). Yet, it does so at the expense of framing satire as 'venting frustrations that might otherwise be expressed in political action' (Freedman, 2008, p. 163; see also Griffin, 1994, p. 157). Sceptics are, therefore, concerned that

> *while the catharsis of satire can soothe the pain of the audience, it often runs the danger of just providing catharsis without spurring the politicians or society to change their ways. (Njoya, 2017; see also Hart, 2013, p. 357; Webber, 2013, p. 147)*

The worry is that '[b]y allowing anger and indignation to vent themselves in laughter, rather than build into action, satire may be a substitute for, not a summons to, revolution' (Nokes, 1987, p. 17).

However, such concerns are unwarranted. The catharsis model of satire is associated with the relief theory of humour, which most scholars dismiss as rooted in an outdated hydraulic understanding of emotion (Carroll, 2014, p. 38; Martin, 2006 p. 58). The idea that humour or satire releases pent-up nervous energy or emotions – like a safety valve releases steam – is not consistent with contemporary theories of humour (see Evans, 2003, pp. 55–60). If humour affords a feeling of relief, it is by priming our cognitive faculties for effort by introducing incongruities which, when we get the joke, dissolve into nothing; as a result, our mind is cognitively unburdened and a sense of levity follows (Carroll, 2014, p. 41).

Still, despite its inaccuracy, the catharsis model hints at an interesting conflict between satire's political and therapeutic affordances. This conflict resonates with the genre's central tension between critique and entertainment. Collingwood (1938) introduces a catharsis theory to distinguish entertainment from magic (see Chapter 2). Whereas magic stimulates emotions like anger or fear for their practical release into everyday life, entertainment arouses emotions for the enjoyment of the release itself (Collingwood, 1938, p. 78).

On Collingwood's model, a joke arouses a feeling of puzzlement which dissipates as we get the punchline, producing a sense of levity which we enjoy for its own sake. Similarly, fear and excitement usually contribute to our survival as part of fight-or-flight responses – but in thrillers or horror films, we enjoy these emotions for their own sake. Still, pace Collingwood (1938), entertainment is not 'a device for the discharge of emotions in such a way that they shall not interfere with the concerns of practical life' (p. 78). Although we do not run out of the cinema when we watch a horror film, anxious feelings may well linger as we walk home in the dark. For example, many people have reported continued uneasiness around clowns, TV sets and even trees as enduring carry-over affects after watching *Poltergeist* (Cantor, 2004, p. 290).

Hence, Collingwood's catharsis model offers no further support for the idea that satire completely discharges emotions that otherwise could contribute to political action. Nevertheless, Collingwood's account does capture the idea that entertainment is enjoyed for its own sake and is unconcerned with practical life. This idea resonates with entertainment's function as diversion and escapism (Katz & Foulkes, 1962; McQuail, Blumler, & Brown, 1972). The intuitive upshot of this idea is that engrossment in entertainment for its own sake can take our mind off practical concerns. Yet, doing so is morally suspicious because it risks distracting us from serious matters altogether, like social injustice.

Therefore, catharsis theories ultimately contribute to refocusing the problematics of satire as therapy, but do not resolve it. Although satire sets out to critique, satirists often frame their satire as therapy for the limits of critique. Intuitively, entertainment has therapeutic affordances which stand to alleviate the limits of critique, because it is divorced from practical concerns and we enjoy it for its own sake. Yet, there is a risk that engrossment in entertainment distracts us from moral commitments, but not because it purges the emotions required for political action – since the therapeutic affordances of entertainment cannot be meaningfully understood as emotional catharsis. We, therefore, need a better understanding of how entertainment works, especially in satire, and how it can contribute to coping with the limits of critique without stimulating moral apathy.

CONCLUSION

Satire does not cure a sick world but helps us to cope with it. Although critique is indispensable, its political impact is limited, as are our resources for critique. This situation introduces neurotic perfectionism and depression as mental health challenges. We, therefore, need coping strategies to deal with suffering that we cannot alleviate, and to which we may even be complicit. Satirists have often framed their satire as a therapy in this challenging situation, which resonates with the fundamental conflict in our lives between the care for others and care of self. According to Dan Perkins, satire is a 'two-pronged assault', a kind of outrage checked by laughter, which advocates the need for critique while helping us to cope with its limits. In the next chapter, I investigate in more detail how satire serves as a resource for good mental health because its purpose to entertain offsets mental health challenges associated with its purpose to critique.

4

THE SOLACE OF ENTERTAINMENT

INTRODUCTION

Rather than a cure for the socio-political ills of the world, satirists typically frame the genre as a coping strategy in a world that is sick beyond full recovery. In this chapter, I develop a conception of satire as therapy framed around the solace of entertainment, which provides pleasurable aesthetic engrossment that lifts our mood and helps to sustain meaning in an absurd world. Satire does not purge distressing emotions altogether but alleviates them in a complex process that negotiates between political action and good mental health. The genre's significance is that its central tension between critique and entertainment serves as a coping resource to negotiate the existential conflict between care for others and care of self. Good satire gets the balance right by avoiding the Scylla of political apathy and the Charybdis of mental health problems.

COPING

According to the transactional model, coping processes 'alter a troubled person–environment relationship' and consist of 'cognitive and behavioural efforts to manage specific external or internal demands (and conflicts between them) that are appraised as taxing or exceeding the resources of the person' (Lazarus, 1991, p. 112). Coping involves a reappraisal (often continually) of the initially troubled person–environment relationship, until the stressors are either satisfactorily addressed or 'chronic stress' occurs, which continues physiological and psychological disturbance (Folkman, 2008, p. 5).

Satire typically addresses a troubled person–environment relationship, as satirists expose social injustices that they do not have the resources to resolve.

This situation, which follows from the limits of critique, is emotionally distressing – and I hypothesise that satire contributes to coping by alleviating this distress. Satire could contribute to coping in different ways. First, satire could function as problem-focussed coping, which 'refers to efforts directed at solving or managing the problem that is causing distress' (Folkman & Moskowitz, 2000, p. 650). Problem-focussed coping involves planning and harnessing resources to 'change the actual relationship' so 'there is no longer a problem and subsidence of the emotional distress should follow' (Lazarus, 1991, p. 112).

Satire is sometimes a stimulus for problem-focussed coping. As argued in Chapter 2, satire can emotionally stimulate or sustain political action to oppose social injustice. For example, the Trump Baby blimp serves to rally support around political causes that oppose Trump's policies. However, political action often does not completely end social injustice, while our resources to sustain critique are also not endless. These limits of critique also entail the limits of problem-focussed coping, which necessitates a different kind of coping through satire, that is, emotion-focussed coping.

Emotion-focussed coping 'change[s] only the way in which the relationship is attended to (…) or interpreted' (Lazarus, 1991, p. 112). Although emotion-focussed coping strategies 'do not change the actual relationship, they change its meaning, and therefore the emotional reaction' (Lazarus, 1991, p. 112). In other words, emotion-focussed coping strategies aim to regulate and ameliorate our distressed response to a troubled person–environment relationship (Biggs, Brough, & Drummond, 2017, p. 353; Folkman & Moskowitz, 2004, p. 751).

Instead of overcoming the limits of critique, which is indeed impossible, satire could contribute to emotion-focussed coping by changing how we feel about our moral imperfection and limited political impact. Such coping is consistent with the wry irony displayed by satirists like Margaret Atwood or the makers of *South Park* in coming to terms with the limits of critique (see Chapter 3). However, framing satire as emotion-faced coping introduces some immediate concerns about its effectiveness.

Emotion-focussed coping is generally considered less effective and adaptive than problem-focussed coping – and is even associated with poor mental health (Folkman & Moskowitz, 2004, p. 747). The maladaptive reputation of emotion-faced coping is enforced by scientific nomenclature like 'escape and avoidance' (Biggs et al., 2017, p. 354), which is linked to strategies like alcoholism and drug abuse (Folkman & Moskowitz, 2004, p. 752).

Concepts like 'escape' and 'avoidance' are also closely associated with the function of entertainment in the tradition of uses and gratification theory

(Katz & Foulkes, 1962). Scholars in this tradition argue that entertainment functions as 'diversion' by providing 'emotional release' and 'escape from the burdens of problems' (McQuail, Blumler, & Brown, 1972, p. 155). As such, entertainment introduces risks associated with 'chronic escapism' and 'addiction' (Huta, 2017, p. 19), including video game addiction (Plante, Gentile, Groves, Modlin, & Blanco-Herrera, 2019) and binge-watching (Riddle, Peebles, Davis, Xu, & Schroeder, 2018).

Al Gini (2017) argues that

> *jokes can serve as a temporary reprieve and antidote to the tribulations of life. To paraphrase satirist Christopher Buckley, humor, like alcohol, at least makes our problems and other people momentarily less troublesome. (p. 48)*

Similarly, Stephen Colbert wonders whether the stress-relieving function of satire is comparable to 'alcohol', which is 'relaxing at first, but your blood pressure actually goes up again the next day' (Marchese, 2019).

However, we should not conflate different kinds of emotion-focussed coping strategies. Although both are routinely identified as emotion-focussed coping, seeking emotional support is obviously more adaptive than problem drinking (Folkman & Moskowitz, 2004, p. 751). Moreover, whereas 'escapist flight' into substance abuse is always maladaptive, emotional 'distancing' can helpfully take our mind of a situation that is beyond our control (Folkman & Moskowitz, 2004, p. 752). This distinction is crucial when framing the affordances of satire as emotion-focussed coping in a situation where nothing (more) can be done. In other words, to cope with the insoluble limits of critique, it would be adaptive for satire to introduce distance through entertainment.

Moreover, distancing typically involves positive emotions, which in turn can contribute to restoring and replenishing other coping resources (Folkman, 2008, p. 12; Folkman & Moskowitz, 2004, p. 766). In the case of satire, our resources for problem-focussed coping are limited; we cannot devote ourselves to political action unabatedly. Therefore, by restoring our resources for problem-focussed coping, satire's affordances as emotion-focussed coping could contribute to sustaining political action in the long run. Hence, distancing through entertainment can complement, if not support, satire's moderate political affordances as critique. Emotion-focussed coping, therefore, does not automatically equal political apathy.

Nevertheless, as discussed, we cannot hope that political action will completely resolve all injustice. Satire addresses a permanently troubled person–environment relationship. In this situation, we can combat chronic stress and associated (mental) health problems by finding positive meaning in life (Folkman, 2008, p. 11). Folkman (2008) specifically highlights how 'even under the most dire circumstances', aesthetic activities like 'enjoying a good movie, or watching a beautiful sunrise' can provide 'a positive moment' (p. 11). In other words, aesthetic appreciation cannot only contribute to coping by instilling positive emotions, but also support 'meaning-focused coping' by introducing a more positive perspective on our situation (Folkman, 2008, p. 6).

One meaning-focussed coping strategy that is particularly relevant in the context of satire is humour, which can function as 'positive cognitive restructuring' (Zautra, Sheets, & Sandler, 1996). In the next chapter, I argue that humour (and irony) in satire can contribute to reframing our perspective on a world that is sick beyond full recovery. For now, I focus on how entertainment, as an aesthetic experience, generates positive emotions and constitutes a 'positive meaningful event', by instilling joy in an absurd world which may otherwise appear devoid of value (Folkman & Moskowitz, 2004, p. 766).

AESTHETIC EXPERIENCE

Aesthetic experiences are a key resource for coping with Nietzsche's difficult truth that there is suffering which we cannot alleviate, and to which we may even be complicit (see Chapter 3). In his discussion of absurdity, Albert Camus highlights that Nietzsche (1955) himself proposes that 'we have art in order not to die of the truth' (p. 69). Nietzsche's point is 'that we possess art so that we can possess the truth and not perish of it' (Williams, 2001, p. xix). Still, it is more precise to say that *aesthetic experiences* are (generally) valuable to cope with the limits of critique, and although these experiences are primarily associated with art, they also characterise the appreciation of nature and activities like cooking and sports (see Kupfer, 1983).

Although there is no consensus about the nature of aesthetic experience, one account that makes minimal commitments characterises it as

> *experience derived from attending in a discriminating manner to forms, qualities or meaningful features of things, attending to these for their own sake or for the sake of a payoff intrinsic to this very experience. (Stecker, 2010, p. 45)*

For example, we derive aesthetic experiences by attending to the harmonious form of a painting, the vibrant quality of its colours or its witty take on a subject.

Aesthetic experiences are puzzling because they are autotelic (we engage in them for their own sake). Hence, although we care about the correctness of our aesthetic judgements, we are not satisfied by simply adopting the correct view of an expert (Nguyen, 2019). A museum guidebook may inform us that a painting is harmonious, vibrant and witty – and we may indeed believe it – but we are clearly missing the point if we do not experience it for ourselves. Similarly, when reading a whodunit, we want to know who the perpetrator is, but flicking through to the final chapter, or looking up the answer online, clearly defeats the point of the activity (Nguyen, 2019, pp. 20–21).

According to C. Thi Nguyen (2019), the purpose of aesthetic appreciation is to engage in 'the various aesthetic activities of perception and investigation for the sake of our *involvement in the activity* of seeking correct judgements' (p. 11, my emphasis). Nguyen (2019) argues that the motivational structure of aesthetic appreciation is similar to playing games (pp. 15–23). We play games to win, but winning is not what really matters; playing is (unless we play for money or other extrinsic rewards). Games involve the voluntary attempt to overcome unnecessary obstacles in pursuit of a seemingly pointless goal (Suits, 2014). Crossing a line or putting a ball in a net is pointless by itself. Yet, when there are rules that make these goals more difficult to achieve, the activity becomes intrinsically interesting.

Consider football, a game which introduces unnecessary obstacles to put a ball into the back of a net, including a goalkeeper (who is the only player allowed to use their hands) and rules like offside. As a result, skill (or luck) is now required to score a goal, which makes the game exciting to play. Similarly, Nguyen (2019) argues that establishing our own aesthetic judgements, without deferring to others, is intrinsically worthwhile because it 'involves pursuing a goal inside certain restrictions' (p. 11). For example, although we can be guided by the analysis of an art critic who labels Mondrian's *Broadway Boogie-Woogie* as unusually dynamic for his style, the point of aesthetic appreciation is that we experience its pulsating vibrancy for ourselves.

That said, aesthetic appreciation need not be exceedingly difficult to be intrinsically rewarding. Take the aesthetic appreciation of watching football. When I plan to watch a recording of a game (because I am busy during the live coverage), I restrict my access to my favourite sports website during the day, to avoid seeing the final score. I want to find out the result for myself by watching the game, not because this is difficult, but because '[w]hat is crucial, especially from the aesthetic point of view, is *how* the score/win is made, not *that* it is made' (Kupfer, 1983, p. 121, original emphasis). In other words, although I want to find out who wins, what I am really after is appreciating the gracefulness of some players, the grit and determination of others, or the unexpected comeback after a suspenseful pursuit.

The motivational structure of aesthetic experience has valuable affordances for coping with an absurd world, as intuited by Nietzsche. Concretely, aesthetic practices like watching sports can become 'a strategy of secular re-enchantment' (Gumbrecht, 2009, p. 150). The aesthetic appreciation of sports may itself appear absurd because its goals (like crossing a line or putting a ball in a net) are pointless 'from life's perspective of necessity' (Welsch, 2005, p. 142). Yet, the point is that '[t]he aesthetic attitude requires that we "distance" ourselves a bit from such realistic, everyday concerns' (Kupfer, 1983, p. 134). Hence, aesthetic engrossment can distance us from a world which is itself absurd (because insoluble suffering exists) by instilling meaning through an intrinsically valuable experience.

Aesthetic experience is a valuable coping resource because it provides distance from practical concerns. As an autotelic experience, aesthetic engrossment contributes to meaning-focussed coping, because it is intrinsically meaningful, irrespective of how we appraise our practical situation outside that experience. Moreover, the positive emotions associated with aesthetic engrossment can contribute to emotion-focussed distancing. As Jenefer Robinson (2020) explains, aesthetic engrossment can support emotion-focussed coping by distancing us from our worries; out at sea, I can 'turn my attention to the creamy whiteness of the fog in order to avoid thinking about its perilous aspects' (p. 209).

Nevertheless, we should not overlook aesthetic diversity and assume that all aesthetic experiences contribute to coping in the same way. One indication of aesthetic diversity is the traditional distinction between fine art and entertainment. According to this distinction, entertainment is mere 'agreeable art', whereas art 'makes more demands on the intellect but offers deeper satisfactions' (Stecker, 2010, p. 80). In this sense, entertainment is like art, but 'lack[s] some pertinent defining features, features that also separate artistic excellence from mediocrity' (Korsemeyer, 2004, p. 112).

This distinction between art and entertainment, which runs parallel to the separation between high and low culture, remains influential. For example, Wolfgang Welsch (2005) explains that professional sports may be appreciated aesthetically, but 'cannot claim the same highbrow status as art' and remain 'somewhat distrusted as a "show for the amusement of the entertainment society"' (p. 137). If we momentarily ignore political issues of cultural status and distinction, there clearly is an intuitive difference between aesthetically appreciating a game of football and a classical concerto. This intuitive distinction between entertainment and other aesthetic experience may signal a relevant difference between coping affordances, which matters to my investigation, given that satire is a genre with the purpose to critique and *entertain* (and not some other aesthetic purpose).

ENTERTAINMENT

Research in psychology has established that not all aesthetic experiences have the same impact on our mood, which is a contributing factor to mental health (Robinson & Knobloch-Westerwick, 2016, pp. 65–66). As discussed, if we cannot successfully cope with the limits of critique, depression looms, which is a mood disorder (Godderis, 2000, p. 173). To regulate mood, the Mood Management Theory (MMT) outlines that people 'avoid entertainment genres that prolong discomfort associated with a negative mood and seek genres that return them to good spirits' (Robinson & Knobloch-Westerwick, 2016, p. 66).

The MMT provides a useful avenue for distinguishing between the coping affordances of entertainment and other aesthetic experience. According to the MMT, entertainment helps to manage arousal levels (a spectrum of psychological and physiological alertness) by regulating between too much arousal (stress) and too little arousal (boredom) (Robinson & Knobloch-Westerwick, 2016, pp. 66–67). Such arousal regulation is linked to 'enjoyment' (Sherry, 2004, p. 330) and promotes wellbeing in the hedonic sense of seeking pleasure and avoiding pain (Huta, 2016, p. 15).

However, critics of the MMT argue that audiences do not just have 'hedonic motivations' to engage with entertainment media; they do not always seek the simple 'enjoyment' afforded by 'amusement', 'thrill' or 'suspense' (Bartsch & Oliver, 2016, p. 82). Instead, audiences also have 'eudaimonic motivations' which guide 'appreciation of more serious types of entertainment' (Bartsch & Oliver, 2016, p. 82). Such media engagement offers 'eudaimonic rewards such as deeper insight, social connection, and personal growth' (Bartsch & Oliver, 2016, p. 89).

Eudaimonic motivations and rewards can explain why audiences watch films about the Holocaust, like *Schindler's List*, which Anne Bartsch and Tilo Hartmann (2017) call 'both [an] intellectual and emotional challenge' (p. 37). They argue that 'entertainment media are used by individuals not only to relax and to improve their mood but also to experience a sense of challenge, meaningfulness, and personal growth' (Bartsch & Hartmann, 2017, p. 30). Such eudaimonic rewards, including long-term contributions to meaning-focussed coping, may well explain why we 'put ourselves through' difficult and upsetting films (Bartsch & Oliver, 2016, p. 87).

The distinction between eudaimoinic and hedonic motivations is reminiscent of the distinction between art and entertainment. Therefore, I doubt that media which only offer eudaimonic rewards really constitute 'entertainment'. Granted, there is an intuitive distinction between 'the hedonic perspective that applies to light, superficial, or pleasurable media experiences' and 'the eudaimonic perspective [which] focuses on content that is more appropriately characterized as heavy, profound, or serious' (Bartsch & Hartmann, 2017, p. 32). Yet, we should not conflate entertainment media (which can be heavy, profound or serious) with entertaining experiences (which are *not* heavy, profound or serious).

For example, *Schindler's List* is directed by Stephen Spielberg, produced by his production company Amblin Entertainment in California and distributed by Universal. There is, therefore, no denying that *Schindler's List* is a 'Hollywood film', and, for this reason, 'entertainment' (see Berliner, 2017). Nevertheless, it would be counterintuitive for somebody to call *Schindler's List* a deeply 'entertaining' film. Similarly, as opposed to classical music, blues and folk are entertainment media, but it does not follow that songs about the horrors of slavery, like Billie Holiday's 'Strange Fruit' or Bob Dylan's 'No More Auction Block', set out to 'entertain'.

In this respect, Richard Shusterman (2008) argues that 'not all valuable [aesthetic] experience need be pleasurable' (p. 82). He too appeals to eudaimonic motivations when arguing that the '[e]xperiences of disturbing shock, fragmentation, disorientation, puzzlement, horror, protest, or even revulsion that contemporary artworks often aim to arouse can be [aesthetically] valued for the novel feelings and thoughts they provide', which 'enrich our vision of the world beyond the artwork' (Shusterman, 2008, p. 81). Clearly, we would not call the challenging aesthetic experiences associated with contemporary art 'entertaining' – and I do not think we should even in traditional contexts of entertainment (like Hollywood or popular music).

There is a crucial difference between 'entertainment media' and aesthetic experiences which are 'entertaining'. Typically, entertainment media primarily set out to entertain (i.e. deliver a specific kind of aesthetic experience). Yet, sometimes, media are classified as entertainment because of contextual reasons, rather than aesthetic ones – as in the case of *Schindler's List*. What satire sets out to achieve, as a genre with the purpose to critique and entertain, is a specific kind of aesthetic experience, which is well captured by the hedonic model of media appreciation.

By contrast, the eudaimonic model of media appreciation really applies to aesthetic experiences that are *not* entertaining. Moreover, this model risks misidentifying and undervaluing entertainment as 'intellectually undemanding'

(Bartsch & Oliver, 2016, p. 81) and 'superficial' (Bartsch & Hartmann, 2017, p. 32). According to Bartsch and Hartmann (2017), hedonic rewards such as 'fun' and 'suspense' do not present 'cognitive challenges' (p. 32). Yet, this cannot be accurate. Just consider the complex plotlines and story worlds of 'quality TV' like *Game of Thrones* or *Dark*, which are clearly suspenseful, or the crafty reflexivity of comedies like *Rick and Morty* or *Community*, which are clearly fun.

The relevant distinction between entertainment and other media cannot be that entertaining experiences are not cognitively challenging. Rather, the crux is that entertainment introduces a challenge which is just 'right'. According to John Sherry, '[t]asks that are too easy result in boredom, whereas tasks that require more skill than the participant possesses can induce anxiety' (Sherry, 2004, p. 332; see also Berliner, 2017, pp. 15–32). Instead, (successful) entertainment stimulates a 'flow state' which 'is realized when there is a balance between the difficulty of the task and the skill of the participant' (Sherry, 2004, p. 332).

The concept 'flow' was introduced by the positive psychologist Mihaly Csikszentmihalyi (1990) to denote an 'autotelic experience' which 'lifts the course of life to a different level' (p. 69). Flow constitutes an emotional state of 'engrossment or absorption', which is part of a larger cluster of interest-related aesthetic emotions (Fingerhut & Prinz, 2020, p. 232). Interest is a contemplative emotion which arises when we feel that we can cope with the challenge of novel and complex stimuli (Silvia, 2005). Flow, specifically, involves a perfect match between our skills and the degree of novelty or complexity. Therefore, an activity which involves 'the application of skilled performance' really feels as if it was 'effortless' (Csikszentmihalyi, 1990, p. 54).

According to Sherry (2004),

> *[e]njoyment of media has many of the same aspects of flow: focused concentration, loss of self-consciousness, a sense that one is in control of the situation, distortion of temporal experience, and the experience of the activity as intrinsically rewarding. (p. 336)*

Many media are explicitly designed to stimulate flow for their targeted audience. For example, quality TV like *The Wire* or *The Sopranos* serve as flow artefacts for an 'exclusive club' of media literate audiences, who expect a certain level of complexity – but not to the degree of, say, David Lynch's *Mulholland Drive*, with its unsolvable plot (Sherry, 2014, p. 335). Similarly, casual games like *Candy Crush* or *Angry Birds* purposefully become more difficult to match players' increasing skill as they progress through the levels.

However, not all aesthetic engagement stimulates flow. Some aesthetic experiences are far from effortless. According to Jenefer Robinson (2020),

> *the most valuable aesthetic experiences are often perceptually or cognitively demanding, as when we follow the score of a late Beethoven quartet or figure out the theme of a late Henry James novel (p. 205, emphasis removed)*

Such media differ from entertainment because they introduce purposefully difficult challenges for relevant experts. By contrast, appreciating the complexity of a series like *The Wire* or *The Sopranos* is really supposed to be comfortable for the intended audience.

Moreover, unlike flow, not all aesthetic experiences require that '[w]e give ourselves over so that the work takes control of our responses' and 'we somehow "lose ourselves"' (Fingerhut & Prinz, 2020, p. 232). For example, art films often prevent such absorption because they are deliberately ambiguous – even for their intended specialist audiences. Concretely, director Lars von Trier prefers 'that his films remain difficult and opaque' and argues that 'a film should be like a stone in your shoe' (Bell, 2005). This metaphor is revealing, because all sorts of activity can stimulate flow, including walking for miles without realising the time. Yet, we will hardly lose ourselves when we walk with a pebble in our shoe.

Arthouse cinema, especially 'extreme cinema' (Frey, 2016), serves as an example of 'anti-entertainment'. Director Michael Haneke claims 'that the purpose of his filmmaking is to "rape" the viewer into a critical spectatorship', which is why critics explain that 'the experience of watching his films seems stressful rather than entertaining' (Frey, 2016, p. 25). Similarly, when critics questioned the ethics of Michael Winterbottom's *The Killer Inside Me* – by calling it 'the most disturbing film of the year' – he retorted that, '[s]urely what would be immoral would be for the violence to be entertaining or acceptable?' (Frey, 2016, p. 26). Interestingly, although extreme cinema often claims a similar critical purpose to satire, these films explicitly do not set out to entertain.

Flow helps to distinguish entertainment from other aesthetic experiences, but it does not by itself define entertaining experiences. According to Sherry (2005), 'entertainment' involves 'emotional pleasure' (p. 330), which he characterises in terms of flow, as a concept that 'account[s] for the pleasure found by immersion in everyday activities' (p. 331). Yet, interest-related emotions like flow are 'empirically dissociable from pleasure' (Fingerhut & Prinz, 2020, p. 229). This distinction matters, because whereas Sherry (2005) rightfully equates 'entertainment' and 'enjoyment' (p. 328), not all media that stimulate flow are intuitively pleasurable and, therefore, not always entertaining.

Consider *Three Identical Strangers*, a documentary about identical triplets who were separated at birth and by sheer coincidence meet in later life. Critics have called it both 'compelling' and 'one of the year's most shocking documentaries' (Nevins, 2018). The documentary is compelling because its plot releases and withholds information in a way which is designed to keep audiences 'on the edge of their seat'. Yet, although compelling, *Three Identical Strangers* is also shocking, and not pleasurable, because it is tinged with negative emotions. Specifically, the controlled release of information cultivates a sense of dread for what the film is yet to reveal.

For example, while two brothers feature as talking heads from the beginning of the documentary, the third brother is conspicuously absent. The documentary intentionally withholds information about the reason for his absence, which contributes to flow: we are compelled to find out why. Yet, as the documentary progresses, so too intensifies a dreadful sense that something terrible happened – and it did (the third brother committed suicide). Although negative emotions like suspense and fear actively contribute to entertainment in genres like thrillers and horror (see Berliner, 2017, p. 7), dread is typically not pleasurable (see Brown, 2019) – and we would be hard-pressed to say that our dreadful suspicions about the fate of the third brother are 'entertaining'.

The point is not that non-fiction media cannot be entertaining. *Louis Theroux*'s *Weird Weekends*, in which the documentary maker meets porn stars, professional wrestlers, and UFO seekers is purposefully entertaining, often despite tackling serious issues. Similarly, Jon Ronson's gonzo journalism often addresses disturbing topics, like psychopathy, but a book like *The Psychopath Test* is also permeated by a sense of wit – which is why it is promoted as 'entertaining' and comes with a guarantee that we will 'zip merrily through it' (Ronson, 2011, back cover endorsements).

However, although compelling, *Three Identical Strangers* does not make us merry. The documentary's many plot twists keep us engrossed, but it would be counterintuitive to label our emotional engagement as pleasurable or enjoyable. Each new bit of salient information reveals that the plight of the triplets is far worse than we could have assumed. By the end of the film, it transpires that they were part of a larger-scale and covert research project that purposefully separated identical twins and triplets to monitor their development in different socio-economic contexts. As one of the brothers acknowledges in the film, such research would not have been out of place in Nazi Germany.

Crucially, while the gradual reveal of this information makes for a fascinating documentary, we would be hard-pressed to call it an entertaining experience. Similarly, entertaining impulses are completely absent from Louis Theroux's *Saville*, a compelling investigation of how sexual predator Jimmy Saville misled an entire nation, including Theroux himself, during decades of sexual abuse. These revelations may be transfixing, but they are equally horrific. Hence, although these documentaries keep us on the edge of our seats, it would be counterintuitive to say that we feel entertained if we are not having fun.

Hence, apart from stimulating flow, entertainment must also involve pleasurable and enjoyable affects (see Sherry, 2005). These aesthetic pleasures follow from the mental processing of sensory stimuli provoked by the character, content or structure of media – like an aptly composed shot in a film (Berliner, 2017, p. 7). Nevertheless, although not all aesthetic experience is pleasurable (see Fingerhut & Prinz, 2020), some aesthetic experiences are pleasurable but not entertaining. For example, René Wellek and Austin Warren (1966) imply a distinction between art and entertainment by arguing that 'the pleasure of literature (...) is a "higher pleasure" because pleasure in a higher kind of activity' (p. 31).

This conception of a 'higher pleasure' is linked to a traditional understanding of aesthetic experience as involving 'pleasurable emotions' derived from a 'positive assessment' of art (Robinson, 2020, p. 212, emphasis removed). Typical emotions associated with entertainment – such as amusement, suspense, or horror – are not usually considered aesthetic emotions in this narrow sense (Robinson, 2020, pp. 218–219). Instead, traditional aesthetic emotions are derived from contemplating 'the form or structure of an artwork and how that structure molds the content of the work, if any' and serve to promote 'the pleasurable contemplation of the artwork' (Robinson, 2020, p. 213).

Aesthetic pleasure in the traditional sense arguably involves a 'higher' pleasure than enjoying a suspenseful game of football, because it is derived from a more reflexive contemplation of form (in relation to content). Experiencing suspense during a game of football involves some basic level of cognition (e.g. understanding that there are only fifteen minutes left to play, which poses a real challenge to score the two more goals required for victory). By contrast, traditional aesthetic pleasure would involve metacognition about the form of football as a game that makes suspense possible (like contemplating the beauty of the offside rule).

Such reflexive pleasure is not altogether alien to appreciating entertainment. We may well enjoy a suspenseful game of football even more because we appreciate how it results from a complex dynamic between the opposing team formations. Still, without those 'base' pleasures like suspense, watching football games would unlikely count as entertainment. Similarly, consider the crafty rhetoric in a satirical joke by Stewart Lee, targeting moral bankruptcy in British politics during the early 2010s:

> *Now in the 1980s, the Labour Party believed that the poor, who did not deserve to be poor, should be helped by the rich, who did not deserve to be rich. Meanwhile, the Conservatives thought that the poor, who deserved to be poor, should not be helped by the rich, who deserved to be rich. And that is the 1980s explained. It's very different today. Today, both the main parties believe that the poor should be tied up in a bin-bag and thrown into a canal. (Lee, 2014)*

Successful uptake of Lee's joke depends, in part, on appreciating how he makes a poignant political point through a crafty use of an antimetabole, a classical rhetorical device whereby a phrase is repeated in reverse order. Hence, appreciating Lee's joke involves a 'higher' aesthetic pleasure, which derives from contemplating form in relation to content. Still, although such appreciation requires skill, it is hardly supposed to introduce a difficult cognitive challenge for Lee's savvy audience. Moreover, despite his shocking assessment of British politics, the joke sets up an incongruity which is clearly designed to be amusing. As amusement, Lee's satire instils a sense of pleasure at a more 'base' level of aesthetic engagement, which makes it entertaining and helps to take the edge off his despairing political analysis.

By contrast, anti-entertainment media, like Gaspar Noé's extreme film *Irréversible,* are intentionally designed as an unpleasant struggle. The film is infamous because it contains a brutally explicit and violent nine-minute rape scene. It also 'includes strobe lights engineered to induce epileptic seizures and sounds at frequencies designed to cause head aches' (Frey, 2016, p. 25). Clearly, as opposed to Lee's satire, *Irréversible* is not pleasurable in any straightforward sense, nor does seek to soften the blow of its disturbing content.

This not to say that *Irréversible* is without aesthetic merit. For one, we can aesthetically appreciate how its complex plot unravels backwards, starting with the end of the story. Therefore, each scene takes us one step back in time, which means we know early on that a rape has happened and spend a significant part of the film in dreadful anticipation of that fateful event. Further, although being forced to witness the brutal sexual assault in a single long take is likely to fill us with abject disgust, we can also appreciate the boldness of Noé's directorial choice, which makes us critically reflect on topics like misogyny, fate and humanity.

Irréversible invites aesthetic appreciation of how its intricate form shapes its message. Still, given the content of that message, it would be counterintuitive to say that aesthetically appreciating *Irréversible* constitutes a 'pleasurable contemplation of the artwork' (Robinson, 2020, p. 213). There are no real reasons to watch *Irréversible* if our motivations are purely hedonic (i.e. maximising pleasure and minimising pain). Instead, we must be driven by eudaimonic motivations, including wanting to challenge ourselves, re-examine our view of humanity or pondering the nature of brutality. The crux is that we do not watch films like *Irréversible* for fun (unless our spectatorship is perverse), but 'to *improve* us' (Suits, 2014, p. 232, original emphasis).

By contrast, entertainment is not edifying, nor does it serve some other serious purpose (see Berliner, 2017, p. 1). Instead, entertainment cultivates 'anti-seriousness', which explains why it is traditionally suspicious in 'a society that both considers leisure and pleasure to be secondary and even inferior to the businesses of producing and reproducing' (Dyer, 1992, p. 2). From this perspective, all art and aesthetic experiences are suspicious. Much like when we play games, appreciating art involves spending resources (like perceptual discrimination) on pursuing pointless goals (like establishing the elegance of a moving body) which could otherwise be put to serious use (like distinguishing benevolent from malevolent moles) (see Nguyen, 2019, p. 24; Suits, 2004, p. 225).

However, at least art serves to edify us, while entertainment just distracts us from the serious business of life. The anti-seriousness of entertainment can be traced at least as far as Plato's *Phaedrus* (1973; see Shusterman, 2003, p. 294). In *Phaedrus*, Socrates introduces an analogy that distinguishes 'between the farmer's serious business and what he might do in a different spirit' (p. 276c), more specifically 'in a holiday mood by way of diversion' and as a 'pastime' which gives 'pleasure' (p. 276b). Whatever 'higher' aesthetic experience we derive from watching *Irréversible* and *Schindler's List*, the crux is that we do not engage with such media in a 'holiday mood by way of diversion'.

MENTAL HEALTH

Entertainment can be meaningfully distinguished from other kinds of aesthetic experience. As predicted by the MMT, mood is a crucial factor that supports this distinction. Since a positive mood contributes to health and wellbeing, the MMT outlines a specific direction for framing the affordances of entertainment as emotion-focussed coping. Specifically, entertainment can alleviate negative moods like stress, anger or fear, which may occur as responses to situations that exceed our resources or are outside of our control (Robinson & Knobloch-Westerwick, 2016).

In this respect, during the COVID-19 crisis and lockdown, the British National Health Service (NHS) advised people to 'not stay glued to the news', do 'things you enjoy' and 'keep [y]our mind active' (NHS Staff, 2020). Entertainment successfully meets these requirements because it is comfortably challenging, pleasurable and engrossing. Of course, other coping strategies are at least equally important; among others things, the NHS also recommended to '[l]ook after your body', '[s]tay connected with others' and '[t]alk about your worries' (NHS Staff, 2020). Nevertheless, entertainment has its role to play, which is consistent with its classical affordance of 'diversion' and 'escape from the burdens of problems' (McQuail et al., 1972, p. 155).

Moreover, philosophers like David Hume (1896 [1739]) intuitively identify entertainment as a coping strategy against 'philosophical melancholy and delirium' – a state of mind that occurs when we feel emotionally unhinged as a result of rationally pondering a problem that 'reason is incapable of dispelling' (p. 269). Hume (1896 [1739]) describes a situation of complete existential disruption – 'Where am I, or what?' – in which he imagines himself 'in the most deplorable condition imaginable, inviron'd with the deepest darkness' (p. 269).

Fortunately, Hume (1896 [1739]) outlines an easy way out of his existential despair, that is,

> *some avocation, and lively impression of my senses (…). I dine, I play a game of backgammon, I converse, and am merry with my friends; and when after three or four hours' amusement, I would return to these speculations, they appear so cold, and strain'd, and ridiculous, that I cannot find in my heart to enter into them any farther.* (p. 269)

In a word, Hume's coping strategy for philosophical melancholy is 'entertainment' – and, by now, it should be clear why.

Although aesthetic experiences like shock and disturbance are certainly valuable, perhaps even as contributions to meaning-focussed coping, they are not appropriate to divert Hume from his existential despair. What he needs is something to lift his mood, not an invitation to continue pondering the darker aspects of life. Hence, if we were to recommend him a film, *Irréversible* is out of the question. Moreover, after all that philosophical contemplation, Hume's cognitive resources are clearly already stretched to their limits. Therefore, even if intellectual effort contributes to the significance of aesthetic experience, Hume is wise to leave James Joyce's *Finnegans Wake* for another day.

Instead, Hume finds solace in pursuits like playing backgammon. If he lived today, we might as well suggest he plays a game of *Candy Crush* to 'Swipe the stress away' (King Staff, 2012). The crux is that entertainment, like playing games, has valuable coping affordances that introduce distance from mental despair. Entertainment involves pleasurable challenges that produce flow, which not only diverts from philosophical melancholy, but instils life with autotelic meaning.

These coping affordances of entertainment are particularly valuable to deal with the limits of critique. The fact that there is suffering which we cannot alleviate, and to which we may even be complicit, can make life seem absurd. In this situation, we risk feeling out of tune with our environment, which can provoke feelings of depression (Godderis, 2000, pp. 175–176). The therapeutic force of entertainment is that it provides us with a visceral entry for reconnection.

Much like Hume, Simon Blackburn (2003) argues that '[m]eaning comes with absorption and enjoyment, the flow of details that matter to us' (p. 70). Hence, if someone is 'sickened by the human carnival, he needs a change of government, or a tonic, or a holiday, rather than an argument' (Blackburn, 2003, p. 64). Although critique indeed often involves pursuing a change of government, the limits of critique imply that political action cannot alleviate suffering completely. We could, therefore, resort to medicinal tonics, including antidepressants, to lift our mood. Yet, if what really counts is autotelic absorption in the flow of details – enjoyed in a 'holiday mood by way of diversion' – Hume is right to look in the direction of entertainment.

Of course, playing *Candy Crush* all the time is not a good idea. For one, while emotion-focussed and avoidant coping strategies are often initially adaptative to regulate our mood, overdependency is clearly maladaptive (see Biggs et al., 2017, p. 355). For example, there is some evidence that playing video games to cope with stress and anxiety may be a contributing factor in video game addiction (Plante et al., 2019). Therefore, advocates of eudaimonic media appreciation are right to warn about 'immediate gratification without regard to potential negative outcomes in the longer run' (Bartsch & Oliver, 2016, p. 87). Sustainable coping with feelings of existential disconnection will clearly involve complementary coping strategies, like physical activity or talking therapy.

Apart from health concerns, the risk of overdependence on entertainment also poses a moral problem. Blaise Pascal (1910 [1670]) worries that we may completely lose ourselves in 'diversions' and ignore the serious business of life altogether. Pascal (1910 [1670]) considers the human condition as permeated by an existential misery from which we constantly seek to escape. According to Pascal, 'so frivolous is he [man], that, though full of a thousand reasons for weariness, the least thing, such as playing billiards or hitting a ball, is sufficient to amuse him' (p. 55). For Pascal, such autotelic engrossment in entertainment is not a welcome coping strategy, but an impediment for self-reflection.

Similarly, Bernard Williams (2001) is concerned that Hume's proposed 'carelessness and inattention' risks developing moral apathy in face of the suffering we cannot alleviate, and to which we are complicit (p. xvii). According to Williams (2001), there is one 'very natural' way of coping with the limits of critique, which is to 'forget that the horrors exist' (p. xvii). Not unlike Pascal, Williams (2001) worries that we risk losing ourselves in 'a pleasantly undemanding and unreflective way of live, a dazed but adequately efficient consumerism' (p. xiv). This risk is not just theoretical.

The entertainment industry offers exactly the kind of distractions associated with a dazed consumerism. Moreover, although the pleasurable distraction of entertainment contributes positively to mood management, this experience is by itself antithetical to critical reflection. Therefore, sceptics decry that satire's entertainment ultimately stimulates cynicism, because it only distracts us from issues that demand political action (see Webber, 2013). However, we should not throw out the baby with the bathwater. In moderation, aesthetic engrossment in entertainment can help us cope with the limits of critique. Satire is significant exactly because it negotiates such moderation by combining this aesthetic solace of entertainment with a moral commitment to critique – although this combination does make the genre ambiguous (see Chapter 1).

SATIRE

Satire's ambiguous central tension between critique and entertainment does not follow from a general conflict between seriousness and diversion. The holiday mood associated with entertainment is not incompatible with the serious business of life. In fact, the purpose of holidays is exactly to rejuvenate us for future work. Similarly, philosophers like Montaigne highlight the value of entertainment as restorative relief, while Richard Shusterman (2003) argues that entertainment can 'sharpen sensitivity of perception' and stimulate 'finer sensibility for new insights' (p. 296).

Moreover, the famous adage of the Roman satirist Horace – that good poetry should combine the useful and agreeable (*utile dulci*) – has resonated far beyond satire (Wellek & Warren, 1966, p. 30). There are many media that combine edification and entertainment (or, put differently, eudaimonic and hedonic affordances). For example, we consider it a virtue if edifying media, like documentaries, combine education and entertainment. Many of us surely also appreciate that museum cafés sell ice creams, so we can have an enjoyable break in between perusing galleries.

However, if the aesthetic pleasures of entertainment are similar to eating ice cream, they are not appropriate in all serious contexts. Take protest marches, for example. There is disagreement about whether Pride parades are really protests or parties. If Pride is all about celebration, ice creams trucks would surely contribute to the party atmosphere. Yet, if Pride really serves to protest patriarchal injustices that contribute to the continuing suffering of the LGBT+ community, eating ice creams is out of place. How could we justify having a party when we should be angry about injustice and suffering? As Bernard Suits (2014) puts it, '[p]laytime comes *after* we save civilization' (p. 534, original emphasis).

Satire is ambiguous because it involves playtime during a rescue mission. There is a conflict between critique, which demands political action, and the aesthetic pleasures of entertainment, which we pursue in a holiday mood by way of diversion. For example, *The Wire* is a realistic crime drama set in Baltimore, which not only reveals the plight of marginalised communities ravaged by drugs, but also serves as a satirical indictment of the 'Orwellian' system that perpetuates social injustice in post-industrial and neoliberal America (Alvarez, 2009, p. 8). Nevertheless, despite its committed critique, actress Sonja Sohn (detective Kima Greggs) explained that 'she was often self-conscious [about] making entertainment, however serious, out of such material' (Alvarez, 2009, p. 46). Sohn, who grew up in similar subsidised housing projects as represented in *The Wire*, felt 'bother[ed]' because the series turned 'a plague' into 'entertainment' (Alvarez, 2009, p. 47).

This unease, which also characterises our moral lives, is central to satire's ambiguity. The previous chapter outlined how satire negotiates a tension between the care for others and care of self. We need to be critical, otherwise we become morally apathetic. Yet, if we devoted ourselves unabatedly to critique, we would compromise our mental health. We, therefore, need to live with suffering that we cannot alleviate and to which we may even be complicit, which is 'uncomfortable' (Blackburn, 1998, p. 232). The same discomfort underpins satire's central tension between critique and entertainment. In satire, entertainment serves to provide solace for the limits of critique, but at the expense of acknowledging its painful implications.

In the previous chapter, I compared satire to a Sisyphus labour and wondered how satirists cope with the limits of critique. The answer is now clear. As Jonathan Swift puts it, '[w]hen you are melancholy, read diverting or amusing books' (Turner, 1986, p. xii). Swift himself hailed the value of 'Amusements, because they preserve my temper as exercise does my Health' (Turner, 1986, p. xii). Of course, satire does more than just entertain. According to Swift, while satirists pursue their own 'private Satisfaction, and Pleasure', they also prompt 'Men of Genius and Virtue, to mend the World as far as they are able' (quoted in Pollard, 1970, p. 73) – even if satire 'will only serve to vex Rogues' but 'not amend them' (quoted in Elkin, 1973, p. 86).

Fortunately for Swift, satire soothes the limits of critique by design, exactly through the entertaining experiences which he himself dearly valued as a resource for mood management. In this respect, Peter Steele identifies 'the confluence of apparently contradicting impulses' in Swift's satire (1978, p. 2). According to Steele, Swift's 'entire career can be described as a partnership of "a clown and preacher"' (1978, p. v). Crucially, this confluence of critique and entertainment has therapeutic benefits for both satirists and their audiences. As James Sutherland (1958) argues, as far as satirists preach to change the world, '[i]t is fun for the preacher, and fun for the congregation' (p. 25). Satire's 'pleasure' is, therefore, not just 'a means of relief for [the satirist's] own outright feelings', but also a coping resource for their audiences (Sutherland, 1962, p. 154).

The coping affordances of entertainment help to explain why satirists are typically modest about their political impact. According to Jon Stewart, if audiences

> *take anything away [from satire], I would imagine it would be that you can have a view of the world that is informed by absurdity or humor that still allows you to feel like you are connected to it. But I don't know that there would be much more than that. (RFE/RL Staff, 2009)*

Stimulating our connection to an absurd world may indeed not seem like much if we narrowly frame satire's significance in terms of political impact. However, given how vital existential connection is to sustain our mental health in a troubling socio-political environment, satire's true significance lies elsewhere (see Godderis, 2000, 175ff).

Although satire has genuine, but modest political affordances, the genre does not cure the ills of the world. Instead, good satire helps us to cope with a world that is sick beyond full recovery. Matthew Hodgart (1969) argues that 'true satire demands a high degree both of commitment to and involvement with the painful problems of the world and a high degree of abstraction from the world' (p. 11). According to Hodgart (1969), satire 'usually offers us a travesty of the situation, which at once directs our attention to actuality and permits an escape from it', because it provokes 'delight at the creation of a beautifully absurd figure' (pp. 11–12). Similarly, I argue that the delight of entertainment provides solace in face of the limits of critique, which is necessary to sustain good mental health in a troubling socio-political environment.

Satire's central combination of critique and entertainment entails that the genre has specific coping affordances which other critical media lack. Consider the dystopian drama *Years and Years*, in which a series of catastrophic events unfold in the near future, including a nuclear attack, economic collapse, authoritarian regimes which enforce racist and homophobic laws, concentration camps for immigrants, career obsolescence due to technological developments, floods and other climate-related crises (the extinction of staple foods like bananas is the new normal) and dirty bomb terrorism. In its critique of the present, *Years and Years* introduces a string of frightfully plausible near-future disasters.

The dystopian prediction of *Years and Years* unfolds around the lives of the intergenerational Lyons family. The Lyonses used to think politics was boring; now they are mostly frightened. *Years and Years* taps into a sense of socio-political anxiety which James Poniewozik (2019) identifies (somewhat disparagingly) as the feeling that 'there's a lot of crazy stuff going on these days'. Yet, he also acknowledges that if you are the kind of person who already thinks modern life is unprecedentedly stressful, '"Years and Years" is not the escape for you' (Poniewozik, 2019).

The dystopian series' aesthetic force is that '[s]o many of the little fearful aspects of *Years and Years* ring true. They come together to form something persistent in the pit of your stomach' (MacInnes, 2019). *Years and Years* is persistently unsettling, even if it is not altogether without hope. In the final episode, ordinary citizens finally manage to unite and stand up to political fascism. Still, an unsettling ambivalence remains. There is no sign that bananas will become available again, while the emotional damage sustained along the way is simply too severe for a truly happy ending.

The series' most devastating moment is the death of Danny Lyons, when trying to smuggle his Ukrainian boyfriend Viktor into the UK, after a long displacement due to anti-gay laws across Europe. There is no ultimate emotional payoff for the mounting suspense we experience as Danny and Viktor attempt to cross the Channel in a small and overcrowded inflatable boat. Suspense quickly turns into dread – surely, something will go wrong! – and later shock, as the camera slowly pans to reveal Danny's dead body on the British coast. Although Viktor survives, he must now live with his own guilt, alongside the grief of the Lyonses and, in some cases, their resentment.

Rotten Tomatoes states that

> Years and Years *scathingly critiques the present with a nihilistic projection of the future, leavening the devastating satire with a buoyant sense of humour and characters who are easy to become invested in. (RT Staff, 2019)*

However, I disagree that *Years and Years* exhibits satire's buoyancy or the hedonic payoff of entertainment. The series' comedy is character-driven; we laugh with the characters, because they have a good sense of humour, which strengthens our attachment and ultimately deepens our devastation as their situation deteriorates. The humour in *Years and Years* may add a sense of humanity, but not fun. Instead, in order to cope with its near-apocalyptic vision, the series forces us to dig deep in our eudaimonic resources (the hope that humanity will prevail, family and love will see us through or that people will ultimately do the right thing).

By contrast, although satire often shares some of *Years and Years*' emotional ambivalence, it offers aesthetic experiences that serve to lift our mood. For example, the humour in Stewart Lee's satirical assessment of British politics in the early 2010s – like his clever use of antimetabole – helps alleviate the particularly dire political assessment (that the main parties in British politics would rather kill than help the poor) (see above). But humour is not the only entertaining (and soothing) resource of satire. Just consider Jimi Hendrix's satirical performance of the American national anthem at Woodstock, in protest to the Vietnam War.

Hendrix' guitar solo distorts the tunes and associated lyrics of 'The Star-Spangled Banner' to critique how American patriotism has been mutilated by warmongering. His instrumental performance ironically comments on the anthem's first stanza, which recounts how the American flag at Fort McHenry withstood bombardments by the British during the War of 1812 (Key, 1814). Hendrix first signals his satirical intent with an abrupt drop in pitch, which bleakly undercuts the anthem's dignified admiration for 'the broad stripes and bright stars' which have remained 'gallantly streaming' despite a 'perilous fight'.

Hendrix continues by mangling the anthem's serene description of 'the rockets' red glare, the bombs bursting in the air'. Instead, we hear a screeching thunder that evokes the sound of a rocket launching and exploding, followed by high-pitched, almost bestial screams of pain, and the low distortion of material destruction. The distortion of the anthem then warps into the opening chords of 'Taps', the bugle call commonly played at military funerals by the US Armed Forces. The ironic allusion to the military casualties in the Vietnam War continues to reverberate, until Hendrix seamlessly leads his band into an up-tempo version of their record chart hit, 'Purple Haze'.

As a satire, Hendrix's 'The Star-Spangled Banner' critiques the immoral American involvement in the Vietnam War by ironically juxtaposing patriotic idealism to hawkish imperialism. Nevertheless, while the evocation of

B-52s dropping bombs over Vietnam is harrowing as a critique, Hendrix's performance explicitly cues aesthetic admiration for his virtuosic skill as a guitar player. Hendrix is showing off and the audience is supposed to enjoy it. Seamlessly incorporated in the set of a rock concert – in between 'Voodoo Child (Slight Return)' and 'Purple Haze' – Hendrix's performance is not simply designed to critique but also to deliver the kind of unexalted aesthetic pleasures associated with entertainment.

Hendrix's performance of 'The Star-Spangled Banner' captures satire's central ambiguity by serving as a significant moment in the history of both anti-Vietnam War protest and rock music, which are practices with radically different purposes. The performance is ambivalent because we are supposed to feel shock as well as admiration – and it feels wrong to aesthetically admire a performance which confronts us with such shocking suffering. Yet, we should remember that suffering cannot always be alleviated, despite the greatest political efforts. By the time of Woodstock, the Vietnam War had been raging for just under 14 years and would continue for 6 more years, costing the combined lives of over a million people (on both sides). Rather than dismissing aesthetic appreciation of Hendrix's satire as apathetic or cynical, we should, therefore, frame it as a coping strategy that defies the absurd limits of critique through life-affirming entertainment.

CONCLUSION

Satire's central combination of critique and entertainment is no coincidence. Critique has its limits, which introduces mental health challenges like depression. In this situation, entertainment has valuable affordances as a resource for emotion-focussed coping. Entertainment involves pleasurable challenges that produce flow, which not only introduces distance from the limits of critique but instils life with autotelic meaning in a socio-political environment that may otherwise appear absurd. Of course, exclusively seeking entertainment, without the support of other coping strategies, is not an appropriate response to this situation. Nevertheless, entertainment is particularly valuable as a jolt to lift our mood and make life meaningful by reconnecting us with our environment.

Moreover, satire is special because, unlike other entertainment, it combines the therapeutic affordances of entertainment with critique. This combination is ambiguous, because there is a conflict between the demands of critique to alleviate suffering and the pleasures of entertainment, which we enjoy in a holiday mood by way of diversion. Yet, this conflict resonates with a fundamental tension in our lives between the care for others and the care of self. Critique is indispensable, but its impact is limited, and so are our resources. To sustain our own mental health, we need distance from critique, which activities like aesthetic engrossment in entertainment provide. Nevertheless, this situation is uncomfortable because it involves accepting insoluble suffering. In the final chapter, I investigate how comic irony in satire helps us to cope with that discomfort without ignoring it.

5

COMIC IRONY AND NARRATIVE COPING

INTRODUCTION

Satire is a resource for coping with the limits of critique. The genre affords autotelic engrossment in entertainment, which lifts our mood and instils life with meaning in a troubled socio-political world. Nevertheless, satire does not just support emotion-focussed coping by taking our mind off insoluble suffering, but also serves as a resource for meaning-focussed coping by actively reframing how we think about the limits of critique. In this chapter, I specifically focus on comic irony in satire as a combination of emotion-focussed and meaning-focussed coping. We can fruitfully integrate these satirical coping strategies in the stories we develop about ourselves in a world that is sick beyond full recovery.

HUMOUR AND HEALTH

Humour's affordances as emotion-focussed coping are similar to entertainment (see Chapter 4). Enjoying humour induces a pleasurable emotional state of 'mirth' (Martin, 2006, p. 8) or 'comic amusement', which is associated with a feeling of 'levity' (Carroll, 2014, p. 58). Positive emotions like these can introduce distance from negative emotions and restore other coping resources (Folkman & Moskowitz, 2004; see also Kuiper & Cann, 2014, p. 414; Martin, 2004). Humour can also make physical contributions to the coping process because its impact on relaxation (Sliter, Kale, & Yuan, 2014, p. 260), as well as state anxiety and mood, is similar to exercise (Szabo, 2011, p. 158).

However, not all humour has the same impact on our mental health. According to the Humour Styles Questionnaire (HSQ), affiliative and self-enhancing types of humour are adaptive, whereas aggressive and self-defeating humour tend to be maladaptive (Martin, Puhlik-Doris, Larsen, Gray, & Weir, 2003). Several studies have established that depression is negatively correlated to affiliative and self-enhancing humour, but positively to self-defeating humour (Kuiper, Grimshaw, Leite, & Kirsh, 2004; Rnic, Dozois, & Martin, 2016; Tucker et al., 2013). Psychological wellbeing may, therefore, depend as much on cultivating beneficial humour styles as the absence of detrimental ones – although conclusively establishing causal relationships between humour and health is difficult (see Gelkopf, 2011; Martin, 2006, p. 281; McCreaddie & Wiggins, 2008).

In any case, we should not assume that all humour is the same. Rod A. Martin (2004, 2006) explains that humour not only has an emotional and physical dimension, but also a cognitive and social dimension. We should, therefore, make fine-grained distinctions along these dimensions between different kinds of humour, which may impact health differently. For example, Martin distinguishes self-defeating from self-deprecating humour; whereas the former stands to make positive contributions to accepting our imperfections (by not taking ourselves too seriously), the latter involves excessive self-disparagement that is correlated to low self-esteem (Kuiper & Martin, 2016, p. 505).

The cognitive dimension of humour is particularly important when considering its affordances to cope with a troubled person–environment relationship. Specifically, we should distinguish comedy which acknowledges the troubled relationship from comedy which ignores it. In this respect, critics speculate that classic 'comfort TV' like *Friends* is popular among young audiences who are 'yearning for a more innocent time' (Godwin, 2019). In the fictional world of *Friends*, even a halfwit like Joey Tribbiani can easily afford a spacious apartment in New York, and most conflicts are happily resolved by the end of the episode. Thus, feelgood sitcoms contribute to emotion-focussed coping by lifting our mood and diverting us from a troublesome world.

By contrast, much contemporary comedy actually confronts the absurdities of life in the twenty-first century through equally absurd humour. Consider *Broad City*, a sitcom about two intelligent but perennially broke young women in New York, who (as opposed to Joey and his friends) constantly worry about rent money. Co-creators Abbi Jacobson and Ilana Glazer acknowledge that the show's absurd humour amplifies experiences from their own lives (Aroesti, 2019). Similarly, meme culture is permeated with jokes that reframe existential despair about the state of the planet or the economy. For example, millennials often share ironic memes to counteract the stereotype that previous generations had it much harder (e.g. we are spoiled with avocado toast and lattes, while our parents had to make do with homeownership in central London).

This kind of humour is still entertaining and, therefore, has emotion-focussed coping affordances by cultivating diversion through aesthetic engrossment. However, humour which does not ignore but rather reframes a troubled person–environment relationship also contributes to meaning-focussed coping by reinterpreting that relationship itself. In other words, humour cannot only indirectly support coping with a troubled person–environment relationship, by shifting our attention elsewhere, but also directly, by shifting our perspective on the relationship itself.

HUMOUR'S COGNITIVE SHIFT

There is a consensus that humour can shift our understanding and appraisal of a troubled person–environment relationship because when we find something funny, it cannot be threatening (Demjén, 2016, p. 20; McCreaddie & Wiggins, 2008, p. 589). Amusement can stimulate a cognitive reappraisal of a stressful situation (Kuiper, Martin, & Olinger, 1993, p. 83) by reframing it from a less-threatening perspective (Kuiper, 2012, p. 484; Martin, 2006, p. 19).

According to Fay Geisler and Hannelore Weber (2010), humour's specific coping affordance is that 'negative experiences are not denied even though construed as less threatening' (p. 447). They stipulate that being amused always involves a situation whereby 'an incident is clearly appraised as harmful' and then reappraised 'as acceptable and normal' (Geisler & Weber, 2010, p. 447; see Veatch, 1998). However, this theory makes counterintuitive presumptions, among which that we should '*care* about linguistic proprieties violated in puns' and 'hold [them] as part of [our] moral systems' – which is why puns are generally enjoyed by 'bookish people' who 'seem to be mildly shocked by a departure from lingu[i]stic norms' (Veatch, 1998, p. 174, my emphasis).

I argue that we need a less counterintuitive theory to understand how humour affords a cognitive shift that makes a situation less threatening. According to Noël Carroll's (2014) incongruity theory, we are amused when we mentally perceive a normative incongruity that flouts our normal understanding of the world (p. 22). In this model, puns are funny because they flout normal communicative practice – but we need not initially appraise such flouting as a threat to the integrity of communication.

Instead, Carroll's (2014) account stipulates that being amused presupposes that the normative incongruity is not perceived as threatening (pp. 26–34). The crux is that not all perceived normative incongruities stimulate comic amusement. A police detective who stumbles on something out of place, like a dead body in the freezer of an ice cream truck, is unlikely to be amused – but rather frightened, puzzled or (if cynical) annoyed at the prospect of more paperwork.

By contrast, being amused by a normative incongruity presupposes that we do not perceive it as frightening, puzzling or annoying (Carroll, 2014, pp. 34–36). Consider an amusing pun like 'The helpers of Santa Claus are known as subordinate Clauses'. Few would appraise this pun as harmful, and someone who did (perhaps out of fear for the secularisation of religious holidays) would not be amused; neither would someone who hated puns or who was interrupted during an important speech; instead, they would be annoyed. 'Getting' the pun also involves appreciating that the incongruity resolves into nonsense; there is no further 'sense' to excavate. (Someone who insists that subclauses could not possibly assist in Santa's workshop has clearly missed the joke.)

Instead, we enjoy puns and other amusing normative incongruities for their own sake and for a feeling of 'levity' that accompanies 'the disappearance of a cognitive demand into nothing' (Carroll, 2014, p. 49). The pleasurable autotelic nature of amusement explains why humour has similar affordances to entertainment as emotion-focussed coping (see Chapter 4). Yet, humour has further affordances as meaning-focussed coping because it can reframe our perspective on a situation that otherwise causes anxiety.

As Carroll (2014) explains, to be amused we 'must regard the incongruity not as a source of anxiety but rather as an opportunity to relish its absurdity' (p. 29). For this reason, '[c]omic incongruities (…) must be non-frightening' or 'what is potentially threatening, frightening, or anxiety producing about them must be deflected and/or marginalized' (Carroll, 2014, p. 30). We cannot be amused if we appraise a situation as threatening. Therefore, much invented comedy stimulates 'comic distance' by introducing conventions to prevent audiences from pondering the potentially troubling implications of jokes; for example, the laugh track in sitcoms signals that we need not worry when someone falls down the stairs (Carroll, 2014, p. 31).

Conversely, we can cultivate comic distance in a situation that is otherwise threating by reframing our appraisal of that situation as amusing. Here, humour does not just distance us from a situation through the diversion afforded by aesthetic engrossment (as all entertainment does), but also by reframing what we think of that situation. Humour can, therefore, contribute to meaning-focussed coping by drawing on our cognitive resources to shift our perspective on a situation that may otherwise appear as hopeless, especially if a troubled person–environment relationship is unlikely to be satisfactorily resolved (see Folkman, 2008; Folkman & Moskowitz, 2004).

A pertinent example of humour's contributions to meaning-focussed coping is Christine-Jane Wilson's cartooning about crossdressing (originally published in the 1980s under the pseudonym Kris, in magazines like

Transgender Tapestry). Wilson explains that 'for many years, before I came to terms with it, being a transvestite was the one thing I thought I would never, EVER be able to laugh about' (correspondence with British Cartoon Archive, original emphasis). In other words, there was a time when fear of social ostracism prevented Wilson from finding humour in crossdressing. This comment highlights that humour is a response-dependent property, meaning that someone will only be amused by a relevant normative incongruity in suitable circumstances (see Carroll, 2014, p. 27).

Throughout her career as a cartoonist, Wilson (2002) was 'always conscious of [her] 40 years of mental turmoil' (p. 25). In response, her cartooning served as an explicit strategy to maintain good mental health in the face of social marginalisation. She explains that

> *[a]ll my life, the main savior of my sanity has been my sense of humor. When I grew depressed, if I feared ridicule or rejection, eventually the funny side would hit me and I'd be able to laugh and climb out of the depression. (...) [By cartooning,] I was able to find humor in being a transvestite. (Wilson, 2002, p. 25)*

She similarly hopes that her cartoons 'give others [fellow crossdressers] a laugh about something they thought they would never be able to laugh at' (Wilson, 2002, p. 25).

Wilson explains that finding humour in crossdressing involves a cognitive shift (being 'hit' by the funny side) which reframes what is threatening as amusing. In her cartoons, Wilson engineers such a cognitive shift by representing crossdressers in funny but awkward situations. Her jokes are structured around normative incongruities involved in two prototypical scenarios. Some cartoons joke about the anxiety of public exposure, like the embarrassment of a crossdresser who is exposed as a child's brother (not mother) by the school gates. Other cartoons make light of the desire for social acceptance, like a crossdresser winning a father's race at their daughter's school event (much to the jealousy of the other dads).

Wilson's cartoons find humour in scenarios where crossdressing is out of the norm. The perceived normative transgression of crossdressing in these scenarios is not inherently amusing – especially to Wilson (2002) herself, who 'spent long enough in the closet to appreciate the worry, tension, and terror' (p. 25). She is acutely aware that crossdressing is 'a sensitive and serious subject' (Wilson, 2002, p. 25). Nevertheless, too much seriousness can become oppressing, especially if it stimulates feelings of alienation or self-hatred in a society that does not tolerate queerness. The therapeutic force of Wilson's cartoons is, therefore, that they introduce a cognitive shift on a troubled person–environment relationship without ignoring it.

At the time of publication, Wilson's cartoons used humour to cope with an insoluble person–environment relationship, since queerness was and would foreseeably remain socially unacceptable. Similarly, humour can reframe past injustices that can no longer be satisfactorily resolved. For example, in her short story 'The Chaos of Angels', LeAnne Howe (2013) uses humour to recount how her Choctaw ancestors were tricked into selling New Orleans to the French. Howe reappraises this traumatic injustice, which can never be rectified, by mocking the French colonist Jean-Baptiste Le Moyne, Sieur de Bienville, for his thick accent, short temper and boorishness.

Nevertheless, although Howe and Wilson both use humour as a coping strategy to reframe an insolubly troubled person–environment relationship, there is a relevant distinction between how their different styles of humour contribute to meaning-focussed coping. The butts of Wilson's jokes are crossdressers like herself, who find themselves in awkward but funny situations. Her self-deprecative humour contributes to coping by reframing those moments of social transgression as harmless (instead of threatening).

By contrast, Howe's (2013) humour is abrasive and directed at an external target, the colonist Bienville, who she nicknames *Filanchi* or 'Our Frenchman, the Nail Biter' (p. 43). This ridicule affords Howe (2013) a symbolic victory in a story where she ultimately needs to accept that 'the joke was on us' (p. 46). Similarly, Demjén (2016) argues that ridicule can be empowering in illness contexts, for example 'downplaying the power of the illness by mocking it and denigrating it to the status of child' (p. 24). The coping affordances of ridicule are consistent with the idea that some kinds of humour involve experiencing a sense of superiority at the expense of a target (Lintott, 2016, p. 365).

Although the HSQ (Martin, Puhlik-Doris, Larsen, Gray, & Weir, 2003) predicts that aggressive humour styles typically correlate with mental ill health, Demjén highlights that ridicule may positively contribute to coping in contexts where a troubled person–environment relationship has a clear cause (like illness). The HSQ is similarly sceptical about self-defeating humour but does acknowledge the positive contributions of self-deprecating humour to put our imperfections into perspective (Kuiper & Martin, 2016, p. 505). Crucially, both ridicule and self-deprecative humour contribute to coping in satire in important ways.

COMIC IRONY AND SATIRE

Ridicule is often central to satire. Consider the Trump Baby blimp (see Chapter 2). Much like cancer patients who find empowerment from their illness by ridiculing their '[n]aughty' stoma bags, protestors can symbolically rob Trump of his political power by ridiculing him as an angry orange baby (Demjén, 2016, p. 25). Similarly, *South Park's* 'The Hobbit' ridicules the short-sighted viewpoints of targets like Butters and Mr Mackey, who fail to spot the obvious falsity of photoshopped female bodies (see Chapter 3). Such ridicule serves as a moral victory for satirists and their audience, which compensates for Wendy's limited political impact (as a stand-in satirist).

Scholars like Dustin Griffin (1994) argue that ridicule affords satirists and their audiences 'a gratifying sense of moral victory to compensate for their status as political underdogs or outsiders' (p. 156). Likewise, satirist Bassem Youssef (2017) argues that satire is 'a great antidote' against the 'fear mentality' cultivated by authoritarian regimes, because '[w]hen you laugh, you are not afraid anymore' (p. 272). These coping affordances of ridicule are sometimes framed as conservative because satirical ridicule is associated with an emotional release that facilitates acquiescence in the status quo (Griffin, 1994, p. 157; Youssef, 2017, p. 238).

However, such pessimism about symbolic empowerment through ridicule is unwarranted. Demjén (2016) has documented how cancer patients gain a sense of empowerment by ridiculing their illness. Such humour use among cancer patients contributes to meaning-focussed coping by facilitating acceptance of a distressing person–environment relationship (see also Lefcourt, 2001, p. 5). Yet, acceptance of a difficult situation does not equal abandoning all hope or effort for recovery. Especially, in illness contexts, the positive emotion of empowerment can emotionally sustain further problem-focussed coping and therapy, like chemotherapy (see Folkman, 2008). There is, therefore, no reason to assume that symbolic empowerment through satire is by default incompatible with political action.

Apart from ridicule, self-deprecative humour also contributes to meaning-focussed coping in satire. Similar to Wilson's cartoons about crossdressers, satirists often poke fun at themselves (or their fictional stand-ins) to deal with the limits of their political impact – from Wendy in 'The Hobbit' to Sparky the Wonder Penguin in *This Modern World*. In interviews and commentary, satirists also typically display a self-deprecating sense of humour to cope with their Sisyphus labour – like Jen Sorensen (2014) who describes satire as worrying 'about how humanity is destroying itself' or Dan Perkins who knows that satire does not 'save the world' but still keeps trying (Rall, 2002, p. 28).

Self-deprecation and ridicule in satire are often jointly expressed through a sense of irony. Importantly, irony is more complex than 'saying one thing while meaning its opposite' (see Carroll, 2014, p. 22). There is a scholarly consensus that communicative irony involves tacitly expressing a dissociative attitude to a defective viewpoint – although scholars disagree about whether ironists 'pretend' to adopt that viewpoint themselves (Currie, 2010) or 'echo' a thought attributed to someone else (Sperber & Wilson, 2012). Settling this disagreement is not important here (instead, see Declercq, 2020). The crux is that when we communicate ironically, we tacitly distance ourselves from a thought attributed to another party.

For example, Jonathan Swift's *A Modest Proposal* ironically promotes a hare-brained scheme to resolve the economic hardship of Ireland's poor (by breeding children to sell as food and commodities to the rich). Swift's irony is more complex than implying the opposite of the scheme; his point is not simply that the Irish should *not* breed children like livestock. Instead, the eponymous modest proposal puts us in mind of similarly ill-judged and cold-hearted population solutions, alongside a general indifference towards the Irish poor among English absentee landlords, from which Swift dissociates himself. This process of attribution and dissociation remains implicit, which explains why it is not immediately obvious that Swift is communicating ironically (or why some readers miss the irony altogether).

Irony is often funny because it exploits a clash between perspectives that can create the right kind of normative incongruity to trigger amusement. *A Modest Proposal* is (darkly) comic because its eponymous proposal advocates a perspective on resolving the Irish economic crisis which flouts how we conventionally make sense of the world. Nonetheless, irony is not always funny. For example, Jimi Hendrix's rendition of 'The Star-Spangled Banner' at Woodstock ironically critiques American hawkishness in the Vietnam War (which is incongruous to the anthem's idealistic patriotism), but it is clearly not amusing.

Still, very often, ridicule and irony go hand in hand in satire. Ironic ridicule perfectly supports satire's central purpose to critique and entertain. Take Margaret Atwood's ironic representation of Professor Pieixoto in the final chapter of *The Handmaid's Tale*. Pieixoto repeatedly indulges in casual sexism, like his redubbing of the 'The Underground Femaleroad' as 'Frailroad' or his deliberate pun on 'the archaic vulgar signification of the word *tail*' in his naming of Offred's eponymous 'tale' (Atwood, 1996 [1985], pp. 312–313, original emphasis). Atwood frames Pieixoto's remarks with a sense of irony – she clearly, but implicitly, dissociates herself from those viewpoints as defective – which is both critical and entertaining.

At the same time, Atwood's representation of Pieixoto serves as a wryly ironic acknowledgement of the limits of critique. Ultimately, the joke is not only on Pieixoto, but also on the satirist and her audience since his casual sexism ironically undercuts the political aim of Atwood's satire. Similarly, in

'The Hobbit', Wendy is the target of a self-deprecative sense of irony when she adamantly exclaims 'I'm not going to rest until photoshopped images are required to be labelled for what they are! Fake! And nothing in this world is going to stop me!' (see Chapter 3). However, the creators of *South Park* immediately undercut her critical zeal by (literally) cutting to the next scene, where Kanye West emotionally blackmails Wendy into stopping her crusade on photoshopped female bodies.

The makers of *South Park* ironically distance themselves from Wendy's unrealistic optimism about her resources for critique and the force of her political impact. This irony is self-deprecative because Wendy's critical mission is clearly analogous to *South Park*'s satire. Hence, such self-deprecative irony helps satirists to reframe the limits of critique by reappraising the limited political impact of their satire. As in Wilson's cartoons, self-deprecative humour helps to reframe an insoluble situation which otherwise risks compromising mental health.

The self-depreciation in *South Park*'s 'The Hobbit' involves a complex interaction between different kinds of irony, which sheds further light on the intricate coping affordances of comic irony. Not only do the makers of *South Park* ironically distance themselves from Wendy's naïve optimism, the editing introduces an extra layer of irony by directly cutting to a scene that undercuts Wendy's statement. Put differently, it is extra ironic that *just* when Wendy exclaims that she will never abandon her critical mission, she immediately does so in the next scene.

This use of editing in 'The Hobbit' creates a fictional representation of situational irony. Situations are ironic when it seems like the universe is frustrating human affairs in an apparently planned and perversely perfect way. For example, there is nothing inherently ironic about politicians having extramarital affairs, but it is ironic when exactly *that* politician, who has made a career out of defending family values, is found cheating around with his much younger assistant. While ironic situations like these are rooted in the contingency of life, their fictional representation is intentionally designed. Concretely, the makers of *South Park* intentionally stage a fictional situational irony by undercutting Wendy's critical zeal immediately after she publicly announced her unabated commitment to critique.

James MacDowell (2016) explains that the fictional representation of situational irony can constitute ironic communication (21ff). He provides the example of depicted situational irony in *Dr Strangelove*, Stanley Kubrick's (1964) satire of Cold War politics. *Dr Strangelove* targets the American and Soviet military policy of Mutually Assured Destruction – commonly abbreviated as MAD (which is itself one of life's perfect ironies). In Kubrick's film, a rogue American general launches a nuclear attack in a fit of paranoia, which (despite top-level diplomacy) cannot be revoked and triggers a Soviet Doomsday device, destroying all life on Earth – including a military and political elite who had hoped to avoid radiation poisoning by spending the next 93 years in abandoned mineshafts.

MacDowell (2016) analyses how Kubrick repeatedly depicts a situational irony by composing shots that explicitly incorporate the military motto 'Peace is Our Profession' – on billboards, letterheads, etc. (pp. 29–32). This was the actual motto of the Strategic Air Command (SAD), which was responsible for Cold War command and controlled most of the US's nuclear weapons. As mayhem unfolds in *Dr Strangelove*, SAD's message of professed peacekeeping is continually ironically undercut, especially when US soldiers open fire at their compatriots during an attack on the rogue general's military base – all within sight of several billboards that proclaim 'Peace is Our Profession'. Clearly, Kubrick's repeated depiction of this situational irony serves as a tacit dissociation from SAD's deception that their core business is peacekeeping.

The fictional representation of situational irony in *Dr Strangelove* both captures and reframes the absurdity of the Cold War and reappraises its existential peril from a less-threating perspective. Thomas Nagel (2012 [1979]) argues that such a sense of irony introduces a comic detachment from insoluble absurdity (p. 20). Similarly, Herbert Lefcourt (2001) argues that a philosophical sense of humour contributes to 'accepting what is uncontrollable' (p. 5). In other words, the comic irony that is typical of satire serves as a resource for satirists to cope with the insoluble problem of a socio-political world that is sick beyond recovery.

However, although comic irony in satire contributes to meaning-focussed coping by introducing distance from an insolubly troubled person–environment relationship, it is not an unreservedly joyful acceptance of everything. Satire does not involve what Lydia Amir (2014) calls 'a constant, serene, and affirmative joy' which 'enables the affirmation of everything' (pp. 280–281). In fact, such an attitude of comic amorality was exactly Juvenal's target in his tenth *Satire*, when he satirised 'the laughing philosopher' Democritus, whom he caricatured as finding 'cause for laughter in *all* human occupations' (Keane, 2015, p. 122, original emphasis).

As Catherine Keane (2015) explains, Juvenal's point is that 'it is difficult to write culturally meaningful satire as a laughing nihilist', for whom everything that happens is really all the same (p. 146). For Juvenal, satire remains a moral act of critique that opposes social wrongness. Apart from Democritus's nihilistic laughter, Juvenal also contrasts satire to the weeping Heraclitus, who acts 'as a symbol of unrelenting melancholy' in face of life's undeniably tragic dimensions (Keane, 2015, p. 125). According to Keane (2015), Juvenal does not outright dismiss either philosophy, but situates the satirist somewhere between the comic amorality of Democritus and the weeping melancholy of Heraclitus (p. 125).

This Juvenalian framework of satire remains relevant to situate the genre's coping affordances in a world that is sick beyond recovery. Satire cannot be unreservedly joyous because it does not ignore insoluble suffering. Nevertheless, coping strategies like comic irony do provide the solace of entertainment and afford a cognitive shift which both serve as a buffer against the mental health challenges associated with the limits of critique. In this manner, comic irony contributes to a complex negotiation in satire between the Scylla of moral apathy and the Charybdis of mental ill health. I now turn to outlining how we can fruitfully adopt and adapt such satirical techniques in our own lives.

NARRATIVE THINKING

Some scholars express scepticism about the health benefits of entertainment media. Rod A. Martin argues that '[s]pending a lot of time laughing at sitcoms on TV is likely to make you less healthy' and 'if there really are any emotional or physical health benefits of humor, they're more likely to come from conversational humor' (Kuiper & Martin, 2016, p. 508). However, the previously introduced Mood Management Theory (MMT) already outlined how audiences can draw on entertainment in the service of mood regulation (Robinson & Knobloch-Westerwick, 2016). Moreover, Martin's scepticism unduly assumes that there is a watertight bulkhead between the comedy we consume and the humour we cultivate in our daily conversations.

Traditional boundaries between media producers and consumers have become increasingly blurred. The availability of relatively cheap digital technologies, like video and graphics editing software, alongside social media as democratic distribution platforms, have enabled virtually everybody to make and share creative content. Meme culture is a particularly good example of how mostly non-professional media users create and distribute comedy online. The 'DIY' comedy of meme culture often does share an absurdist sensibility with professionally produced 'millennial' and 'Gen Y' comedy (Aroesti, 2019). Moreover, films and TV series often serve as source material for comic re-appropriation in memes. Hence, meme culture testifies to how the comedy we consume influences the humour we cultivate in our daily interactions.

Our engagement with entertainment media is fundamentally active. Even the leisurely aesthetic appreciation of entertainment, like Hollywood films, already requires significant cognitive engagement (see Berliner, 2017). Hence, when we laugh at sitcoms, our engagement is far from passive. Yet, sometimes, our media use is especially active, as when we use sitcoms as source material for creating memes. Such active media use can contribute to coping. During the 2020 Covid-19 crisis, various news outlets reported on how media users turned to creating and sharing absurd memes to deal with the existential disruption of lockdown (Bellan, 2020; Paul, 2020). We should, therefore, look beyond media consumption to frame satire's affordances as a coping resource for ordinary media users.

To illuminate how ordinary media users can exploit satire as a coping resource, I introduce a narrative framework. Narratives are artefacts that help us make sense of the world (Williams, 2002, p. 233). Humans have always told myths and folktales to interpret a bewildering and frequently hostile world (Gersie & King, 1990, p. 23). In a psychiatric context, such 'story-making' is regularly framed 'as a life-supporting process, a psychic resource, a defence against futility, emptiness, and formless terror' (Roberts, 1999, p. 13). Similarly, in seminal investigations of illness narratives, scholars like Arthur Kleinman (1988), Arthur Frank (1995) and Rita Charon (2006) have revealed the importance of narrative meaning-making in illness contexts (both for those who give and receive care).

Likewise, satires are (generally) narrative artefacts that introduce techniques that can inform the stories we tell about ourselves in a troubled-socio-political world. The idea that narratives frame our understanding of ourselves and the world should not be conflated with the more extreme claim that our identities or lives are narratives (see Woods, 2011). Narratives are meaning-making artefacts which tell stories that represent events; sometimes these events involve ourselves and our lives, but that does not make them narratives (Goldie, 2012, pp. 154–155). In other words, we should not conflate the value of illness narratives with the idea that illness is a narrative.

Stories create meaning by establishing coherent (and often causal) connections between selected events (Goldie, 2012, 14ff). Hence, a list of information is not by itself a narrative. My GP's health and care report, which lists information about my healthcare, does not tell a story (and, therefore, does not make sense of my illness experiences). By contrast, my diary entries do tell a story, for example, by connecting the depressive feelings I shared with my GP that day to a memory from high school. Stories such as these are narrated from a certain perspective, from which represented events are typically evaluated and imbued with emotional import (Goldie, 2012, 8ff). In my diary entry, I can tell the story of how a short-sighted teacher wrongly accused me of stealing, which now makes me feel both angry and sad.

According to Peter Goldie, 'the narratives that we weave about our lives can profoundly affect how we respond to our past, and how we lead our lives in the future' (Goldie, 2004, p. 117). Such 'narrative thinking' can be expressed through a physical artefact, like a letter (which we share with others) or a diary (which is private), but it can also just involve sequences of thought, feeling and imagination (Goldie, 2012, pp. 4–5). Narrative thinking enables us to take an evaluative perspective on our past and future selves and, thus, arrive at a correlative emotional response about what we did then or should do next (Goldie, 2004, p. 117).

Narrative thinking about ourselves often involves taking a perspective on our thoughts or actions as if we were someone else (Goldie, 2004, pp. 109–111). Therefore, narrative thinking enables us to think through how others see us (like the short-sighted teacher in my diary entry who thought I was a thief). Hilde Lindemann (2001) argues that our sense of personal identity is determined by a complex interaction between how we and others see ourselves (p. xi). Sometimes, our personal identities are damaged by how others perceive us, especially through socially shared understandings in foundational master narratives (Lindemann, 2001, p. 6). In response, Lindemann (2001) argues that we can develop 'counterstories' to challenge and repair our damaged self-understanding (p. 7).

Both Howe's short story about the French colonist Bienville and Wilson's cartoons about crossdressers are examples of how counterstories serve as narrative repair by redressing the damage of harmful master narratives. Howe's ridicule of Bienville contributes to reclaiming a sense of moral superiority in opposition to countless stories in American culture (like classical Westerns) which depict the native tribes as villains and the white settlers as heroes. Similarly, Wilson's cartoons reclaim queerness as an identity that can be playful in response to master narratives which frame it as unnatural.

Counterstories such as these can harness the coping affordances of narrative strategies. Jenefer Robinson (2004) argues that the 'formal or structural devices in literature [can] play the role of coping mechanisms' by reappraising emotionally challenging content (p. 196). For example, Robinson (2004) explains how formal devices like allegory and juxtaposition 'manage' the uncomfortableness of Matthew Arnold's poem 'Dover Beach', so we can appreciate it aesthetically, despite its themes of loss, darkness and sadness (p. 212). She also explains how the plot structure and setting of Edith Wharton's *The Reef* serve as a 'defensive strategy' against the more unpleasant parts of the book (Robinson, 2004, p. 214).

Crucially, these kinds of narrative strategies can be adopted and adapted in the stories we tell about ourselves and the world. According to Lindemann (2001), the stories that contribute to our personal identity contain 'stock plots and character types' that we borrow, often unconsciously, from narratives that circulate in our culture (p. 72). Similarly, Goldie (2004) argues that we may consciously think of ourselves as such-and-such a character from a film, and that the stories we tell about ourselves often borrow from established narrative forms and genres (pp. 116/121/126).

Similarly, I frame satire as a resource for narrative sense-making about what we should do in a world that is sick beyond full recovery. Satires like *The Handmaid's Tale* or *Dr Strangelove* operate like counterstories that reclaim the right to remain 'sane' in a 'mad' world, by exposing master narratives like patriarchal neo-conservatism and Cold War propaganda as 'insane'. Satire introduces various narrative strategies, especially different devices of comic irony, which contribute to coping by reappraising a troubled socio-political world from a less-threatening perspective. We can, therefore, approach satire as a reservoir for coping strategies that we can adopt and adapt in our own narrative thinking.

SATIRICAL COPING STRATEGIES

Narrative thinking about ourselves typically involves an epistemic, evaluative and emotional 'gap' that is akin to experiencing dramatic irony in fiction (Goldie, 2012, p. 106). For example, in *Oedipus Rex*, the audience has a different perspective on the unfolding tragedy than Oedipus himself, because we know from the start that he has killed his father and will marry his mother (Goldie, 2012, pp. 26–30). Similarly, narrative thinking about our past, especially grief, often involves a similar ironic gap (Goldie, 2012, p. 56). As I recount the last moments with my dear friend (before her unexpected accident), I know now what I did not then; therefore, her seemingly trivial jokes have become very significant to me, while the amusement I felt then is now imbued with sadness.

Likewise, our narrative engagement with satire involves negotiating an ironic gap that follows from the limits of critique. Reflexive engagement with satire presupposes earnest critique of social wrongness. Yet, we also know (and the reflexive satirist knows) that there is suffering which we cannot alleviate and to which we may even be complicit. This ironic gap resonates with an insoluble dichotomy between the care for others and the care of self, which we all experience if we take narrative thinking about ourselves seriously in a world that is sick beyond full recovery. Managing this ironic gap through a combination of critique and entertainment is what determines the ambiguity and significance of satire.

Comic irony is one central narrative strategy through which satire negotiates the limits of critique. A wry sense of irony contributes to emotion-focussed coping (by introducing positive emotions and lifting mood through aesthetic diversion) and meaning-focussed coping (by reappraising the troubled person–environment relationship). There are several formal and structural devices through which comic irony is expressed in satire – too many to attempt to list exhaustively here. Instead, I conclude by outlining three significant satirical coping strategies which we can integrate in our own narrative thinking, that is, analogy, reversal and 'ironic characters'.

Analogy is a common strategy in satire to ridicule a target through a corresponding fictional representation, which exploits a central likeness that is typically exaggerated, grotesque or otherwise absurd (see Diehl, 2013). Perhaps the most canonical example of satirical analogy is how Jonathan Swift likens contemporaneous population solutions to his absurd 'modest' proposal. Similarly, *South Park*'s 'The Hobbit' ridicules society's infatuation with unrealistic beauty standards by likening it to the inability of elementary schoolers to distinguish between the real Lisa Berger and her photoshopped image – even when she is standing right in front of them (see Chapter 3).

Ridicule through analogy contributes equally to satire's purpose to critique and entertain. A good analogy serves up the absurdity of a social wrongness by capturing it in a poignant image. For example, *South Park* captures how the warped beauty standards associated with photoshopped bodies perpetuate racism and ableism – by showing how a picture of Nicole, a black cheerleader, is white-washed, while Timmy, who sits in a wheelchair, is stripped of his physical and mental disability. Such poignant analogies stimulate our imaginative faculties and can produce a 'jolt' of insight about how pernicious a situation really is, which can raise our critical awareness or perhaps even inspire us to political action.

Apart from critique, the imaginative use of analogy in satire also contributes to entertainment – as when we see Clyde gleefully striding across South Park Elementary, showing off Lisa's photoshopped image on his phone while holding the real Lisa by the arm. Such an analogy is not just insightful as critique, but also funny. As an aesthetic device, analogy helps us cope with the limits of critique, which are so painfully captured through Wendy's plight (see Chapter 3). The use of comic analogy throughout the episode introduces both a pleasurable diversion from and a less-threatening perspective on the absurd insolubility of Wendy's situation. Crucially, analogy is a satirical technique that we can straightforwardly integrate in our own narrative thinking.

For example, to cope with the government's latest scaremongering, we can liken the behaviour of callous politicians to pathetic schoolyard bullies.

Alongside analogy, reversal is another satirical technique that contributes both to critiquing and to coping with an absurd situation. Satirical reversal shifts our evaluation of a situation from negative to positive, for example through an incongruous plot structure. Consider *Blindboy Undestroys the World,* a TV show in which the Irish satirist Dave Chambers (2018) (aka Blindboy Boatclub) exposes the UK's broken housing system. The show's grammatically incorrect title ironically echoes the heroic assumption that satire could somehow 'unbreak' a broken world. Blindboy also cultivates a wry sense of irony to deal with the limits of critique, especially during a section on an exploitative letting agency in London, which extorts tenants through a host of outrageous hidden charges.

The section starts with Blindboy introducing an exploitative contract from Lifestyle Club London. Instead of 'systematically dissect[ing] this contract by clause' (as an investigate journalist would do), Blindboy instead announces that '[w]e're going to play The Hidden Charges Game Show'. The game consists of two 'contestants' moving into a property of the agency. The winner is the person who ultimately amasses the most hidden charges, for example, for not making their bed (£200), contacting the office out of hours (£25) or using a blow heater (£200). Thus, Blindboy reverses our appraisal of a deeply disturbing situation by turning it into a darkly comic game.

Blindboy wryly jokes that, right from the start, 'the fines increase and the mental health degenerates' – especially when 'depressed Alicia forgets to pay her rent for a week. [The result:] Seven separate fines'. After amassing £990 in fines, Alicia finally decides to leave, but not without having to pay an out-of-season fee (£200). 'Not able to afford it', Blindboy explains, 'she stays in the room and freezes to death. Oh, no! Her corpse is blocking the door and racking up fines. The irony! This is life in 2018'. He then exclaims, 'We have a winner!' and – while glitter falls on Alicia's motionless body – he looks into the camera, pauses, and says: 'satire'.

The story of The Hidden Charges Game Show is extremely bleak – as is its conception of satire. Blindboy's narrative about the London housing crisis should really be plotted as a tragedy. In a tragic plot, Alicia would make the ominous mistake to rent from Lifestyle Club London, for which she would pay dearly with her life. Yet, Blindboy reverses expectations by introducing a rags-to-riches plot, which is darkly comic because the riches are incongruously awful. Through such an incongruous plot structure, Blindboy both captures the absurdity of the seemingly insoluble London Housing crisis and reassesses it from a less-threatening perspective.

Similarly, Kubrick's *Dr Strangelove* comically reverses the appropriate appraisal of Cold War politics in its adaptation of Peter George's thriller novel, *Red Alert*. The plot of both narratives is virtually identical, except that nuclear annihilation is narrowly averted at the end in the novel, but not the film. Kubrick (1963), who explicitly referred to the nuclear arms race as a 'tragedy (which has not yet occurred)', considered that the only appropriate response to the existential absurdity of the Cold War was to turn George's 'completely serious suspense story' into 'a nightmare comedy' (pp. 12–13). This comically incongruous reversal does not imply that Kubrick dismissed the seriousness of the threat. Instead, Kubrick's stepdaughter, Katharina, disclosed that her father was 'terrified' by the prospect of nuclear war – and continuously tried to shelter his children from this anxiety (Brady, 2019).

By the same token, Kubrick's choice to reframe his adaptation of George's novel as a comedy facilitates coping with anxiety by reversing how we evaluate the threat of nuclear annihilation in the fiction. As the events unfold in *Dr Strangelove*, they no longer provoke anxiety in response to impending doom, as they do in *Red Alert*, but rather a wry sense of amusement. Tellingly, Kubrick's film also follows the threat of nuclear war through to its terrifying but logical conclusion, whereas a nuclear disaster is ultimately prevented in George's novel. Here, Kubrick's wry irony serves as an emotional buffer that does permit to fully face the threat of nuclear war without succumbing to outright despair.

Much like *Blindboy Undestroys The World*, Kubrick's *Dr Strangelove* demonstrates the coping affordances of a narrative that incongruously reverses our evaluation of an insoluble existential threat. We too can adopt this strategy by ironically reframing absurd political failures (like climate change or global economic inequality) as incongruous achievements in some ridiculously defective understanding of the world. Such reframing ridicules the absurdity of political ineptitude and helps us cope with anxiety, so that we do not succumb to existential despair in the face of seemingly insoluble threats. This kind of coping does not automatically equal a passive acceptance of the situation but can instead facilitate political action by managing our anxiety. In this respect, if we are consumed by anxiety, we are also unlikely to engage in meaningful political action.

Alongside reversal and analogy, satire's nuanced coping affordances in the face of existential absurdity are perhaps best epitomised by what I call 'ironic characters' (see Declercq 2020). Ironic characters in satire do not themselves communicate ironically in the fictional world but serve as a device in the ironic communication of satirists. They are characters that assert viewpoints that audiences are cued to understand as deficient viewpoints about real-world affairs. In contrast to dramatic irony, satirists do not only intend for audiences to have knowledge that these ironic characters lack, but also to actively dissociate themselves from their viewpoints as ridiculous.

Satirists frequently use ironic characters to ridicule powerful targets, like the American President Merkin Muffley in *Dr Strangelove*, who shows no awareness of Kubrick's prank to name him after a pubic wig. The absurd shortsightedness of the fictious President serves as a comment on the ill-considered policies of the US government during the Cold War. Kubrick communicates ironically by staging situations where the President makes the most cretinous remarks without realising it – as when he tries to break up a fighting US general and Soviet ambassador with the famous words, 'Gentlemen. You can't fight in here. This is the War Room!' Although implicit, Kubrick clearly distances himself from Merkin Muffley's defective viewpoints, as a stand-in for the policies of the US government.

Ironic characters afford a sense of intellectual and moral superiority over satirical targets, but they do not always serve to critique social wrongness. Quite often, satirists introduce ironic characters as stand-ins of themselves, for the purpose of coping with the limits of critique. One example is Chidi Anagonye, the deceased ethics professor in the comedy series, *The Good Place*. Although *The Good Place* is a comedy and not a satire, it does introduce a satirical take on moral perfectionism by ridiculing Chidi's efforts. Chidi always wants to make a morally perfect choice, which makes him look ridiculous because it is a torture for both himself and his environment.

Similarly, satirists regularly mock ironic versions of themselves to deal with their moral imperfection in a world where insoluble suffering exists. Consider Huey Freeman in Aaron McGruder's satirical comic strip (and animated series) *The Boondocks*. Huey may only be a teenager, but – named after Black Panther Party co-founder Huey P. Newton – he is staunchly committed to a 'radical-left black militancy' (Swanigan, 2012, p. 34). Similarly, public perception has often framed McGruder as a 'black socialist' (Swanigan, 2012, p. 29) and 'angry revolutionary' (Rabin, 2005). Nevertheless, McGruder stresses that '[i]t would be inaccurate to say that Huey's opinions are my own' (Carbin, 2001). Most importantly, Huey displays an unabated critical zeal from which McGruder distances himself through comic irony.

On the one hand, Huey's actions in *The Boondocks* resemble McGruder's satirical mission. Typical behaviour for Huey includes telling his grandfather that his dinner fork may well contain traces of radioactive nickel, because the government's policy is that it is 'more cost-effective to recycle than destroy' (McGruder, 2000, p. 127). McGruder argues that '[g]ood satire (...) teaches you how to think critically' and serves to impart 'a message about the lies a society tells itself' (Cavna, 2008). Huey is, therefore, like a satirical gadfly who seeks to sting his environment out of complacency. Nonetheless, as he simply cannot let his grandfather enjoy his dinner in peace, there is something comically ironic about Huey's relentless zeal.

Throughout *The Boondocks*, Huey is the butt of McGruder's ironic characterisation. Whereas McGruder explains that 'revolution is very difficult, and I'm not optimistic for any kind of dramatic change' (Rabin, 2005), Huey often proclaims a palpably absurd commitment to revolutionary ideals. Huey will say things like, 'I want my people to be free!! I will enlighten the masses!! My voice will ring out across the globe and make a difference' – but, ultimately, McGruder (2001) always confronts him with the reality of his limited political impact (p. 33).

Huey is an ironic character because he exhibits a boundless commitment to critique from which McGruder implicitly distances himself. McGruder cultivates a comic irony that introduces a psychological distance from the limits of critique, which is necessary to sustain good mental health in a world that is sick beyond full recovery. By contrast, Huey is unable to distance himself from his ideals and is, therefore, continuously moody, if not depressed. When his friend Jazmine asks about his professional aspirations, Huey responds, 'it would be to dedicate myself totally to the liberation of oppressed people around the globe' (McGruder, 2001, p. 72). Quite poignantly, Jazmine retorts, '[b]ut you're doing that now and you're always miserable!' (McGruder, 2001, p. 72).

Crucially, McGruder's ironic mockery of Huey's radical critique should not be dismissed as cynicism. Satirists like McGruder use strategies like ironic characters to negotiate a more complex balance between critique and mental health – by ironically mocking a deludedly zealous version of themselves. McGruder explains that the world 'seems to be going in a really bad, bad place really quickly, and I don't have the answers. (...) But the continued apathy will only lead to a worse situation for everybody' (Rabin, 2005). Satire like *The Boondocks* is, therefore, not an excuse to acquiesce in the status quo but an attempt to improve the world while coping with its insoluble sickness.

Satirists develop narrative techniques like ironic characters which we can also incorporate as coping strategies in the stories we tell about ourselves and our place in an imperfect world. We too can think of ourselves as an overzealous idealist like Huey Freeman and find amusement in our moral imperfection – and, thus, prevent ourselves from being consumed by an unabated critical zeal. We can engage in counterfactual narrative thinking, whereby we imagine what our lives would be like if we acted like Huey. And as we imagine harassing our family members about radioactive cutlery, we hopefully cultivate a sense of amusement that helps us come to terms with the limits of critique.

Narrative thinking about ourselves is an important resource to manage mental health and guide practical deliberation in an imperfect world. Goldie (2004) highlights the importance of narrative thinking for future planning, especially to think through our own plans as if from an external perspective (pp. 110–114). Similarly, Carroll (2012) identifies the *orientational* role of narrative in deliberating what we ought to do (p. 390, original emphasis). Narrative strategies in satire are, therefore, at the intersection of negotiating between the care for others and the care of self, that is, what we ought to do in the service of critique and how we should act to cope with its limits. Therefore, as narrative artefacts, satire offers us valuable resources for coping with our moral imperfections in an imperfect world.

CONCLUSION

Comic irony in satire contributes to coping not just by introducing positive emotions, but also by cognitively shifting our perspective on the limits of critique. Amusement is caused by the perception of normative incongruities which, among other things, do not frighten us. Hence, feeling amused about a situation that we initially appraised as threatening means successfully reappraising it from a less-threatening perspective. Satire introduces several strategies to reappraise deficient perspectives which may otherwise be experienced as threatening, including analogy, reversal and ironic characters. These deficient viewpoints can be attributed to political opponents, but also ourselves, if we are prone to critical ideals that are ultimately detrimental to our mental health. Hence, satire is a resource that offers us narrative coping strategies that we can adopt and adapt in our narrative thinking about how to live in a world where insoluble suffering exists.

CONCLUSION

This book has addressed three main questions. What is satire? What can it do or not do? And, why should we care about it? I have argued that satires are artefacts that are designed to critique and entertain. Although satire's two central purposes fruitfully interact, the leisurely aesthetic enjoyment of entertainment does sit uneasy alongside critique's moral demands to oppose social wrongness. Therefore, satire is fundamentally ambiguous. Unlike other entertainments, such as playing *Candy Crush* or watching professional sports, satire is not something we engage with just for fun. Yet, as opposed to protest marches or hunger strikes, satire is also not the most devoted form of political action. This ambiguity is purposeful, because satire is a form of critique designed to cope with the limits of critique – by providing entertainment as an aesthetic coping resource.

We should not understand satire's significance narrowly in terms of its political impact, and certainly not as a metaphorical cure for a sick world. Still, we should also not dismiss satire as cynical or politically apathetic. Satire's political impact is best understood as harnessing emotional resources to stimulate or sustain other forms of political action, which have greater political impact. Satire like the Trump Baby blimp is a 'magic' totem which serves as an emotional booster to motivate more impactful forms of critique, like grassroots political activism. These political affordances of satire are genuine, but modest. Therefore, we should not primarily and exclusively frame the genre's significance in terms of its political impact. Otherwise, satire appears less significant than it really is.

Satire's real significance is as a resource for coping with a world that is sick beyond full recovery. Critique has its limits: we do not have endless resources to sustain political action, and even if we did, we would not always achieve political success. Nietzsche's difficult truth is that suffering exists which we cannot alleviate (and to which we may even be complicit). If we cannot deal with these limits of critique, we stand to compromise our mental health – either by falling prey to neurotic perfectionism (if we ignore those limits and try to devote ourselves unabatedly to critique) or by feeling depressed (through existential disconnection from an absurd world where insoluble suffering exists).

Therefore, we need strategies to cope with a world in which the demands of critique continuously exceed our resources. The easiest solution is to distract ourselves from this conflict and forget all about it. In an episode of *Rick and Morty*, Rick Sanchez outlines this exact solution when he tells his grandson, Morty Smith, '[y]our only purpose in life is to buy and consume merchandise' (Roiland & Harmon, 2020). Morty has just bought his grandpa a magic toy train and Rick is overjoyed, telling Morty that

> *you went into a store ... an actual honest to God store... and you bought something. You didn't ask questions or raise ethical complaints. You ... you just looked straight into the bleeding jaws of capitalism and said 'Yes, daddy, please!'.*

Of course, the satirical point is that if we listened to Rick's advice, we would become as cynical and politically apathetic as he is.

Hence, the challenge is to find the right balance between two extremes, that is, boundless care for others (which results in mental health issues) and inconsiderate care of self (which results in moral and political apathy). Satire is a valuable resource for such existential negotiation between the care for others and the care of self. Satire helps us deal with the limits of critique through the solace of pleasurable autotelic engrossment in entertainment, which reconnects us to an otherwise depressingly absurd world. Satirical jokes like Rick's advice to Morty are designed for our aesthetic enjoyment. Therefore, they can lift our mood when the world gives us few other reasons to feel uplifted. Yet, of course, satire does not just divert us. The genre is still a genuine form of critique, which does not let us forget that social injustice exists – and that we should do something about it when we can.

Entertainment in satire contributes to emotion-focussed coping by distancing ourselves from the painful truths revealed by its critique. Crucially, satire does not purge negative emotions like anger and frustration, which could otherwise contribute to political action. Instead, entertainment stimulates pleasurable and positive emotions, which contribute to coping by offering aesthetic distance. Moreover, positive emotions can also restore and replenish resources for problem-focussed coping, which seeks to redress the underlying problem. Without satire, the limits of critique may well grind us down altogether. Therefore, when we laugh at Rick's advice to Morty, we are not just distancing ourselves from the painful and insoluble excesses of capitalism. We are taking a break that may reinvigorate us for further political action. In this respect, even if Rick's metaphorical beast with the bleeding jaws cannot be slayed, we can at least try to wound it.

Moreover, satire is not just an artefact for media consumption, but also a resource that we can adopt and adapt in our narrative thinking. Hence, if we are prone to inconsiderate self-preservation in the face of the limits of critique, we may come to see ourselves like Rick, an ironic character with ridiculously defective viewpoints. Similarly, we can appropriate other satirical strategies, like analogy and reversal, to reassess the limits of critique from a less-threatening perspective. Such narrative thinking is crucial to our sense of identity, moral deliberation and mental health. Stories help us to understand who we are, guide our actions and make sense of the otherwise crushing contingency of life. Therefore, satire is perhaps most valuable as a narrative resource that offers us tools for the stories we tell about ourselves in a world that is sick beyond full recovery.

My investigation of satire's artefactual affordances has concluded that the genre is deliberately designed for the purpose of coping with the limits of critique. I have demonstrated satire's affordances as a coping resource by drawing on methodologies from the humanities, particularly close analysis and philosophical explication. Satirists themselves have often intuited these affordances, by saying that satire keeps them sane (and hoping that the same goes for their audiences). Therefore, a significant aim of my investigation has been to theoretically unpack and support these intuitions. Throughout, I have tried to do so in a dialogue with research from the social and natural sciences when possible (especially the Mood Management Theory and Revised Transactional Model of Coping).

Nevertheless, it is a limitation of my investigation that I have not empirically examined satire's effects (on satirists or their audiences). This limitation is partly deliberate, because I developed this project with the conviction that we first need to establish what satire is and what it is designed to achieve, before we can really conceive of meaningful empirical research. Yet, as a scholar working in the humanities, I also do not have the training, nor the resources to attempt an empirical study of satire's coping affordances. Still, I do hope that my own specialisms have put me in the right place to analyse the nature, affordances and value of satire as a specific artform. I further hope that my study can be an impetus for future empirical research into satire, comedy and mental health (which combines relevant expertise from the humanistic, social and natural sciences).

Perhaps the most significantly underdeveloped area in my study of satire (and comedy) is its social dimension (see Demjén, 2016; Martin, 2004; Sliter, Kale, & Yuan, 2014). Dan Perkins (aka Tom Tomorrow) frames satire as

> *sending out these little smoke signals to let people know that they're not crazy and they're not alone, that there are other people out there who feel the way they do. (Elias, 2003)*

Similarly, Aaron McGruder contends that

> *[t]here is a silent majority that is opposed to the direction of the country and my strip gives them a small outlet every day to feel like they're not crazy. (Younge 2005)*

These comments strike me as a particularly fruitful direction for a future empirical investigation into how satirists and their fans form communities around satire as a resource for coping in troubled socio-political world.

For now, I limit myself to concluding that satire is artefactually designed as a tool for coping with the limits of critique. We all need to find a balance between the care of self and the care for others. If not, we either become politically apathetic or psychologically unhinged in the face of suffering that we cannot alleviate (and to which we may even be complicit). Although satire is not a panacea, it is a tool that we can use to manage this existential discomfort – and, hopefully, I have outlined some ways to do so. Satire's affordances as a tool are not comparable to a safety valve, which mechanically and automatically relieves our despair. Instead, satires are narrative artefacts which incorporate aesthetic strategies that we can adopt and adapt to cope with our moral imperfection in a morally imperfect world.

BIBLIOGRAPHY

Abell, C. (2015). Genre, interpretation and evaluation. *Proceedings of the Aristotelean Society*, *115*(1), 25–40.

Adorno, T. W., & Horkheimer, M. (1944/2002). *Dialectic of enlightenment*. (Trans. Edmund Jephcott). Stanford, CA: Stanford University Press.

Akingbe, N. (2014). Speaking denunciation: Satire as confrontation language in contemporary Nigerian Poetry. *Afrika Focus*, *27*(1), 47–67.

Albrecht, G. (2011). Chronic environmental change: Emerging 'psychoterratic' syndromes. In I. Weissbecker (Ed.), *Climate change and human well-being* (pp. 43–56). New York, NY: Springer.

Alter, A. (2017). Uneasy about the future, readers turn to dystopian classics. *The New York Times*, January 27. Retrieved from https://www.nytimes.com/2017/01/27/business/media/dystopian-classics-1984-animal-farm-the-handmaids-tale.html?_r=0

Alvarez, R. (2004). *The Wire: Truth be told*. Edinburgh: Cannongate.

Amir, L. B. (2014). *Humor and the good life in modern philosophy: Shaftesbury, Hamann, Kierkegaard*. Albany, NY: State University of New York Press.

Aroesti, R. (2019). 'Horrifyingly absurd': How did millennial comedy get so surreal? *The Guardian*, August 13. Retrieved from https://www.theguardian.com/tv-and-radio/2019/aug/13/how-did-millennial-comedy-get-so-surreal

Arrant, C. (2012). Conversing on comics with Matt Bors. *CBR.com*, October 26. Retrieved from http://www.cbr.com/conversing-on-comics-with-matt-bors/

Atwood, M. (1985/1996). *The handmaid's tale*. London: Vintage.

Atwood, M. (2003). Orwell and me. *The Guardian*, June 16. Retrieved from https://www.theguardian.com/books/2003/jun/16/georgeorwell.artsfeatures

Atwood, M. (2012). Haunted by The Handmaid's Tale. *The Guardian*, January 20. Retrieved from https://www.theguardian.com/books/2012/jan/20/handmaids-tale-margaret-atwood.

Barry, J. (1971). *Lenny: A play based on the life and words of Lenny Bruce*. New York, NY: Grove Press.

Bartsch, A., & Hartmann, T. (2017). The role of cognitive and affective challenge in entertainment experience. *Communication Research*, 44(1), 29–53.

Bartsch, A., & Oliver, M. B. (2016). Appreciation of meaningful entertainment. Experiences and eudaimonic well-being. In L. Reinecke & M. B. Oliver (Eds.), *The Routledge handbook of media use and well-being* (pp. 14–33). New York, NY: Routledge.

Baym, G. (2009). *From Cronkite to Colbert. The evolution of broadcast news*. Oxford: Oxford University Press.

Beard, D. S. (2004). Local satire with a global reach: Ethnic stereotyping and cross-cultural conflicts in *The Simpsons*. In J. Alberti (Ed.), *Leaving Springfield. The Simpsons and the possibility of oppositional culture* (pp. 273–291). Detroit, MI: Wayne State University Press.

Becker, M. (2008). I hate hippies: South Park and the politics of generation X. In J. A Weinstock (Ed.), *Taking South Park seriously* (pp. 145–164). Albany, NY: State University of New York Press.

Bell, E. (2005). Lars von Trier: Anti-American? Me? *Independent*, October 21. Retrieved from https://www.independent.co.uk/arts-entertainment/films/features/lars-von-trier-anti-american-me-321010.html

Bellan, R. (2020). Laughing during a crisis: The best coronavirus memes. *Forbes*, March 19. Retrieved from https://www.forbes.com/sites/rebeccabellan/2020/03/19/laughing-during-a-crisis-the-best-coronavirus-memes/

Berliner, T. (2017). *Hollywood aesthetic: Pleasure in American cinema*. New York, NY: Oxford University Press.

Biber, D., & Conrad S. (2009). *Register, genre, and style*. Cambridge, MA: Cambridge University Press.

Biggs, A., Brough, P., & Drummond, S. (2017). Lazarus and Folkman's psychological stress and coping theory. In C. L. Cooper & J. C. Quick (Eds.), *The handbook of stress and health: A guide to research and practice* (pp. 351–364). Chichester: John Wiley & Sons.

Birney, A. L. (1973). *Satiric Catharsis in Shakespeare: A theory of dramatic structure*. Los Angeles, CA: University of California Press.

Blackburn, S. (1986). Making ends meet. *Philosophical Books*, 27(4), 193–203.

Blackburn, S. (1998). *Ruling passions*. Oxford: Oxford University Press.

Blackburn, S. (2003). *Ethics. A very short introduction*. Oxford: Oxford University Press.

Böhmermann, J., host. (2016a). *Neo Magazin Royale*. ZDFneo, March 31. Retrieved from: https://vimeo.com/161272558

Böhmermann, J. (2016b). Liebe Fans des Neo Magazin Royale. *Facebook*, April 16. Retrieved from *https://www.facebook.com/jboehmermann/posts/1174196975946157*.

Boler, M., & Turpin, E. (2008). The daily show and crossfire: Satire and sincerity as truth to power. In M. Boler (Ed.), *Digital media and democracy: Tactics in hard times* (pp. 383–404). Cambridge, MA: MIT Press.

Booklist Staff. (2007). As the world burns: 50 simple things you can do to stay in denial. *Booklist*, November 15. Retrieved from https://www.booklistonline.com/As-the-World-Burns-50-Simple-Things-You-Can-Do-to-Stay-in-Denial-Derrick-Jensen/pid=2347795

Bors, M. (2013). *Life begins at incorporation*. Self-published.

Brady, T. (2019). Armageddon time: How Stanley Kubrick made us laugh at the annihilation of the human race. *Irish Times*, May 11. Retrieved from https://www.irishtimes.com/culture/film/armageddon-time-how-stanley-kubrick-made-us-laugh-at-the-annihilation-of-the-human-race-1.3883776

Branham Bracht, R. (2009). Satire. In R. Eldridge (Ed.), *The Oxford handbook of philosophy and literature* (pp. 139–161). Oxford: Oxford University Press.

Braund, S. M. H. (1996). *The Roman satirists and their masks*. London: Bristol Classical Press.

Bronner, E. (2011). *Critical theory. A very short introduction*. Oxford: Oxford University Press.

Brown, D. W. R. (2019). Dreading the future: Narrative dread in *Better Call Saul* and contemporary television. *NECSUS. European Journal of Media Studies*, *8*(1), 231–248.

Brown, M. (Ed.). (1993). *Horace. Satires I*. Warminster: Aris & Phillips.

Brown, M. (2015). Ai Weiwei's RA show to house weighty remnants from Sichuan Earthquake. *The Guardian*, June 15. Retrieved from https://www.theguardian.com/artanddesign/2015/jun/15/ai-weiwei-ra-show-sichuan-earthquake-chinese-artist-steel-rods

Bybee, C., & Overbeck, A. (2001). Homer Simpson explains our postmodern identity crisis, whether we like it or not: Media literacy after 'The Simpsons'. *Simile: Studies in Media & Information Literacy Education*, *1*(1), 1–12.

Cambridge, E. (2019). Bye bye baby. *The Sun*, June 4. Retrieved from https://www.thesun.co.uk/news/9222160/baby-donald-trump-blimp-popped/

Camus, A. (1955). *The myth of Sisyphus and other essays* (Trans. Justin O'Brien). New York, NY: Alfred A. Knopf.

Cantor, J. (2004). 'I'll never have a clown in my house'—Why movie horror lives on. *Poetics Today*, *25*(2), 283–304.

Carbin, J. A. (2001). Boondocks speaks: An interview with Aaron McGruder. *Alternet*, November 4. Retrieved from http://www.alternet.org/story/11859/boondocks_speaks%3A_an_interview_with_aaron_mcgruder

Cardoen, S. (2017). Herman Brusselmans richt zijn scheldproza naar 'blonde del die weigert pil te slikken' oftewel Anouk. *De Redactie*, June 21. Retrieved from http://deredactie.be/cm/vrtnieuws/cultuur%2Ben%2Bmedia/media/1.3006705

Carroll, N. (2012). *Art in three dimensions*. Oxford: Oxford University Press.

Carroll, N. (2014). *Humour. A very short introduction*. Oxford: Oxford University Press.

Cavna, M. (2008). The interview: 'Boondocks' creator Aaron McGruder. *The Washington Post*, July 22. Retrieved from http://voices.washingtonpost.com/comic-riffs/2008/07/the_interview_aaron_mcgruder.html

Chambers, D. [Pseud. Blindboy Boatclub], creator. (2018). Blindboy undestroys the world. The broken housing system. *BBC*, October 31.

Charon, R. (2006). *Narrative medicine: Honoring the stories of illness*. Oxford: Oxford University Press.

Charrington, M. (2001). Introduction. In *2024*, Ted Rall (pp. 5–6). New York, NY: NBM Publishing.

CNN Staff. (2014). How comedians made net neutrality matter. *CNN*, November 17. Retrieved from https://www.youtube.com/watch?v=aXsYqN8ulbA

Cohen, J. (Ed.). (1975). *The essential Lenny Bruce – His original unexpurgated satirical routines*. London: Panther Books.

Colbert, S., host. (2015). John Oliver doesn't care about Donald Trump. *The Late Show with Stephen Colbert*. CBS, September 13. Retrieved from http://www.cbs.com/shows/the-late-show-with-stephen-colbert/video/9C4A3F78-8492-012E-75E4-214FC748F70C/john-oliver-doesn-t-care-about-donald-trump/

Colletta, L. (2009). Political satire and postmodern irony in the age of Stephen Colbert and Jon Stewart. *The Journal of Popular Culture*, *42*(5), 856–874.

Collingwood, R. G. (1938). *The principles of art*. London: Oxford University Press.

Combe, W. (1777/2010). *The justification: A poem*. Whitewish, MT: Kessinger Publishing.

Condren, C. (2012). Satire and definition. *Humor*, *25*(4), 375–399.

Condren, C. J., Davis, M., McCausland, S., & Phiddian, R. A. (2008). Defining parody and satire: Australian copyright law and its new exception: Part 2 – Advancing ordinary definitions. *Media and Arts Law Review*, *13*(4), 401–421.

Critchley, S. (2001). *A very short introduction to continental philosophy*. Oxford: Oxford University Press.

Crow, D. (2013). South Park: The hobbit review. *Den of Geek*, December 12. Retrieved from http://www.denofgeek.com/us/tv/south-park/231593/south-park-the-hobbit-review

Csikszentmihalyi, M. (1990). *Flow. The psychology of optimal experience*. New York, NY: Harper Perennial.

Cuddeback, L. (2015). From the outside: Jon Stewart, satire, and the catholic church. *Political Theology Network*, August 15. Retrieved from https://politicaltheology.com/from-the-outside-jon-stewart-satire-and-the-catholic-church-lorraine-cuddeback/

Currie, G. (2004). *Arts and minds*. Oxford: Oxford University Press.

Currie, G. (2010). *Narratives and narrators: A philosophy of stories*. New York, NY: Oxford University Press.

Cvetkovich, A. (2012). *Depression: A public feeling*. Durham, NC: Duke University Press.

D'Anastasio, C. (2018). How the 'NPC' meme tries to dehumanize 'SJWs.' *Kotaku*, November 5. Retrieved from https://kotaku.com/how-the-npc-meme-tries-to-dehumanize-sjws-1829552261

Davies, R. T., creator. (2019). Episode 4. *Years and Years. BBC One*, June 4.

Day, A. (2011). *Satire and dissent. Interventions in contemporary political debate*. Bloomington, IN: Indiana University Press.

Day, A. (2013). Shifting the conversation: Colbert's Super PAC and the measurement of satirical efficacy. *International Journal of Communication*, 7, 414–429.

Declercq, D. (2013). The philosophical and ethical significance of humour. *The Simpsons* as humorous ethical truth-telling. *Ethical Perspectives*, *20*(2), 271–298.

Declercq, D. (2018a). A definition of satire (and why a definition matters). *Journal of Aesthetics and Art Criticism*, *76*(3), 319–330.

Declercq, D. (2018b). Can we learn the truth from Lenny Bruce? A careful cognitivism about satire. In I. MacKenzie, F. Francis, K. Bonello Rutter Giappone (Eds.), *Comedy and critical thought*. Lanham, MD: Rowman & Littlefield.

Declercq, D. (2019). Drawing truth differently. Matt Bors' fictional satire and non-fictional journalism. *ImageText 11*(1). Retrieved from http://imagetext.english.ufl.edu/archives/v11_1/declercq/

Declercq, D. (2020). Irony, disruption and moral imperfection. *Ethical Theory and Moral Practice*. Retrieved from https://doi.org/10.1007/s10677-020-10105-z

Degerman, D. (2019). Brexit anxiety: A case study in the medicalization of dissent. *Critical Review of International Social and Political Philosophy*, *22*(7), 823–840.

Demjén, Z. (2016). Laughing at cancer: Humour, empowerment, solidarity and coping online. *Journal of Pragmatics*, *101*, 18–30.

DeRochi, J. (2008). 'What have you learned?' Considering a new hermeneutic of satire in *Family Guy*. *Studies in American Humor*, *3*(17), 35–48.

Dessau, B. (2012). *Beyond a joke. Inside the dark world of stand-up comedy*. London: Arrant.

Dessem, M. (2017). John Oliver eviscerates Donald Trump's ties to Vladimir Putin. *Slate*, February 20. Retrieved from http://www.slate.com/blogs/

browbeat/2017/02/20/john_oliver_eviscerates_donald_trump_s_ties_to_putin.html

Dettmar, K. J. H. (2004). Counterculture literacy: Learning irony with *The Simpsons*. In J. Alberti (Ed.), *Leaving Springfield. The Simpsons and the possibility of oppositional culture* (pp. 85–106). Detroit, MI: Wayne State University Press.

Diehl, N. (2013). Satire, analogy, and moral philosophy. *Journal of Aesthetics and Art Criticism*, *74*(1), 311–321.

Dixon, G. (2008). The uncertain future: Tom Tomorrow [*sic.*]. *The Washington Post*, October 1. Retrieved from https://www.washingtonpost.com/express/wp/2008/10/02/the_uncertain_future_tom_tomoroow/

Donnelly, E. (2014). Seth MacFarlane, sick of being called misogynist, says 'we saw your boobs' was satire. *Flavorwire*, November 13. Retrieved from http://flavorwire.com/488234/seth-macfarlane-sick-of-being-called-misogynist-says-we-saw-your-boobs-was-satire

Döpfner, M. (2016). The freedom of art and satire. *Die Welt*, April 10. Retrieved from https://www.welt.de/debatte/kommentare/article155290190/The-Freedom-of-Art-and-Satire.html

Dyer, R. (1992). *Only entertainment*. London: Routledge.

EA Staff. (n.d.). Emotional support service for Europeans. Existential Academy. Retrieved from https://www.existentialacademy.com/esse/

Ebel, M. (2016). Pupswitzbolds Erklärstunde. *Tages Anzeiger*, May 4. Retrieved from http://www.tagesanzeiger.ch/kultur/diverses/pupswitzbolds-erklaerstunde/story/10714156

Ebert, R. (1974). Lenny. *RogerEbert.com*, November 10. Retrieved from https://www.rogerebert.com/reviews/lenny-1974

Eco, U. (1984). The frames of comic 'freedom'. In T. A. Sebeok (Ed.), *Umberto Eco, V.V. Ivanov, Monica Rector. Carnival!* (pp. 1–10). Berlin: Mouton de Gruyter.

Elgot, J., & Connett, D. (2018). Blue planet gift from Theresa May to remind Beijing of plastic waste. *The Guardian*, January 31. Retrieved from https://www.theguardian.com/environment/2018/jan/31/blue-planet-gift-from-theresa-may-to-remind-beijing-of-plastic-waste

Elias, R. (2003). Tom Tomorrow. *The Progressive*, March 1. Retrieved from https://www.thefreelibrary.com/Tom+Tomorrow.+(The+Progressive+Interview)-a099818450

Elkin, P. K. (1973). *The Augustan defence of satire*. Oxford: Clarendon Press.

Elliott, R. C. (1960). *The power of satire: Magic, ritual, art*. Princeton, NJ: Princeton University Press.

Encyclopedia Dramatica Staff. (n.d.). Meme magic. *Encyclopedia Dramatica*. Retrieved from https://encyclopediadramatica.rs/Meme_Magic

Encyclopedia Dramatica Staff. (n.d.). The great meme war. *Encyclopedia Dramatica*. Retrieved from https://encyclopediadramatica.rs/The_Great_Meme_War

European Journalists Staff. (2019). Monitoring jailed journalists in Turkey. *European Journalists*, February 1. Retrieved from https://europeanjournalists.org/turkey-journalists-in-jail/

Evans, D. (2003). *Emotion: A very short introduction*. Oxford: Oxford University Press.

Farage, N. (2010). *Exert from speech*. Wikiquote. Retrieved from https://en.wikiquote.org/wiki/Nigel_Farage

Faris, R., Roberts, H., Etling, B., Othman, D., & Benkler, Y. (2015). *Score another one for the Internet? The role of the networked public sphere in the U.S. net neutrality policy debate, 2015-4*. Cambridge, MA: Berkman Center Research Publication. http://dx.doi.org/10.2139/ssrn.2563761

Fettis, A., director. (2010). Frost on satire. *BBC*, June 17.

Filipino Times Staff. (2018). Netizens Use 'Winnie the Pooh' pics as unusual way to welcome Xi Jingpin. *Filipino Times*, November 20. Retrieved from https://filipinotimes.net/news/2018/11/20/filipinos-use-winnie-pooh-pics-unusual-way-welcome-xi-jingpin/

Fingerhut, J., & Prinz, J. J. (2020). Aesthetic emotions reconsidered. *The Monist*, *103*(2), 223–239.

Folkman, S. (2008). The case for positive emotions in the stress process. *Anxiety, Stress, & Coping*, *21*(1), 3–14.

Folkman, S., & Moskowitz, J. T. (2000). Positive affect and the other side of coping. *American Psychologist*, *55*, 647–654.

Folkman, S., & Moskowitz, J. T. (2004). Coping: Pitfalls and promise. *Annual Review of Psychology*, *55*, 745–774.

Fowler, A. (1985). *Kinds of literature: An introduction to the theory of genres and modes* (2nd ed.). Oxford: Clarendon Press.

Frank, A. (1995). *The wounded storyteller*. Chicago, IL: University of Chicago Press.

Freedman, L. (2008). *The offensive art: Political satire and its censorship around the world*. Santa Barbara, CA: ABC-CLIO.

Freemuse Staff. (2011). Morocco: Call for solidarity with Mouad Belghouat, known as El Haked. *Freemuse*, June 6. Retrieved from https://freemuse.org/def_art_freedom/morocco-call-for-solidarity-with-mouad-belghouat-known-as-el-haked/

Freudenburg, K. (2001). *Satires of Rome: Threatening poses from Lucilius to Juvenal*. Cambridge: Cambridge University Press.

Frey, M. (2016). *Extreme cinema. The transgressive rhetoric of today's art film culture*. New Brunswick, NJ: Rutgers University Press.

Fritzsche, H. (1934). Dr. Goebbels und sein Ministerium. In H. H. Mantau-Sadlia (Ed.), *Deutsche Führer Deutsches Schicksal. Das Buch der Künder und Führer des dritten Reiches* (pp. 330–342). Munich: Verlag Max Steinebach (Trans. Randall Bytwerk). Retrieved from https://research.calvin.edu/german-propaganda-archive/goeb62.htm

Gallagher, N. (2013). Satire as medicine in the restoration and early eighteenth century: The history of a metaphor. *Literature and Medicine*, *31*(1), 17–39.

Gaut, B. (1998). Just joking: The ethics and aesthetics of humor. *Philosophy and Literature*, *22*(1), 51–68.

Geisler, F. C. M., & Weber, H. (2010). Harm that does not hurt: Humour in coping with self-threat. *Motivation and Emotion*, *34*(4), 446–456.

Gelkopf, M. (2011). The use of humor in serious mental illness: A review. *Evidence-based Complementary and Alternative Medicine*, 342837. https://doi.org/10.1093/ecam/nep106

Geranmayepoura, S., & Besharata, M. A. (2010). Perfectionism and mental health. *Procedia Social and Behavioral Sciences*, *5*, 643–657.

Gersie, A., & King, N. (1990). *Storymaking in education and therapy*. London: Stockholm Institute of Education Press.

Gini, A. (2017). *The importance of being funny: Why we need more jokes in our lives*. Lanham, MD: Rowman & Littlefield.

Godderis, J. (2000). *Kan men een hemel klaren, even zwart als drek? Historische, psychiatrische en fenomenologisch-antropologische beschouwingen over depressie en melancholie*. Leuven: Garant.

Godwin, R. (2019). The age of comfort TV: Why people are secretly watching *Friends* and *The Office* on a loop. *The Guardian*, August 21. Retrieved from https://www.theguardian.com/tv-and-radio/2019/aug/21/the-age-of-comfort-tv-why-people-are-secretly-watching-friends-and-the-office-on-a-loop

Goldie, P. (2004). *On personality*. London: Routledge.

Goldie, P. (2012). *The mess inside. Narrative, emotion, and the mind*. Oxford: Oxford University Press.

Gowers, E. J. (2012). Satire (satura). In S. Hornblower, A. Spawforth, & E. Eidinow (Eds.), *The Oxford classical dictionary* (4th ed.). Oxford. Oxford University Press . Retrieved from https://www.oxfordreference.com/view/10.1093/acref/9780199545568.001.0001/acref-9780199545568-e-5715?rskey=CuN7BK&result=1.

Gray, J. (2005). *Watching with The Simpsons: Television, parody, and intertextuality*. New York, NY: Routledge.

Greenwald, G. (2006). Tom Tomorrow's hell in a handbasket. *Unclaimed Territory*, October 10. Retrieved from http://glenngreenwald.blogspot.co.uk/2006/10/tom-tomorrows-hell-in-handbasket.html

Gregoire, J. (2017). *Meme magic*. Washington, DC: Amazon.

Griffin, D. (1990). Venting spleen. *Essays in Criticism*, *40*(2), 124–135, 131–132.

Griffin, D. (1994). *Satire: A critical reintroduction*. Lexington, KY: University Press of Kentucky.

Grigson, G. (Ed.). (1980). *The Oxford book of satirical verse*. Oxford: Oxford University Press.

Groening, S. (2008). Cynicism and other postideological half measures in *South Park*. In J. A. Weinstock (Ed.), *Taking South Park seriously* (pp. 113–130). Albany, NY: State University of New York Press.

Guardian Staff. (2019). The guardian view on phasing out packaging: Back to the plastic-free future. *The Guardian*, June 4. Retrieved from https://www.theguardian.com/commentisfree/2019/jun/04/the-guardian-view-on-phasing-out-packaging-back-to-the-plastic-free-future

Guerrero, L. A. (2019). *Crazy funny: Popular black satire and the method of madness*. New York, NY: Routledge.

Gumbrecht, H. U. (2009). 'Lost in focused intensity': Spectator sports and strategies of re-enchantment. In J. Landy & M. T. Saler (Eds.), *The re-enchantment of the world: Secular magic in a rational age* (pp. 149–158). Stanford, CA: Stanford University Press.

Habinek, T. (2005). Satire as aristocratic play. In K. Freudenburg (Ed.), *The Cambridge companion to Roman satire* (pp. 177–191). Cambridge, MA: Cambridge University Press.

Hansen, S. (2003). Tomorrow's news, Today! *Salon*, August 15. Retrieved from http://www.salon.com/2003/08/14/perkins/

Hart, R. P. (2013). The rhetoric of political comedy: A tragedy? *International Journal of Communication*, 7, 338–370.

Hendra, T. (1987). *Going too far. The rise and demise of sick, gross, black, sophomoric, weirdo, pinko, anarchist, underground, anti-establishment humor*. New York, NY: Doubleday.

Hi's Eye Staff. (2017). SNL saves our sanity: Satire's role in the time of Trump. *Hi's Eye*, March 24. Retrieved from https://hiseye.org/780/his-eye/snl-saves-our-sanity-satires-role-in-the-time-of-trump/

Higgie, R. (2014). Kynical dogs and cynical masters: Contemporary satire, politics and truth-telling. *Humor*, 27(2), 183–201.

Highet, G. (1962). *The anatomy of satire*. Princeton, NJ: Princeton University Press.

Hodgart, M. J. C. (1969). *Satire*. London: Weidenfeld and Nicolson.

Holbert, R. L. (2013). Developing a normative approach to political satire: An empirical perspective. *International Journal of Communication*, 7(1), 305–323.

Howe, L. (2013). *Choctalking on other realities*. San Francisco, CA: Aunt Lute Books.

Hume, D. (1739). 1896. In L. A. Selby-Bigge (Ed.), *A treatise of human nature by David Hume*. Oxford: Clarendon Press.

Humor Times Staff. (n.d.). Rescue your sanity in the age of Trump with the Humor Times free App! *Humor Times*. Retrieved from https://www.humortimes.com/64569/sanity-trump-humor-times-free-app/

Huta, V. (2016). An overview of hedonic and eudaimonic well-being concepts. In L. Reinecke & M. B. Oliver (Eds.), *The Routledge handbook of media use and well-being* (pp. 80–92). New York, NY: Routledge.

Jenkin, D. (2017). Saving sanity: The role of cartoonists in the real world. *Media Update*, February 16. Retrieved from https://www.mediaupdate.co.za/media/126795/saving-sanity-the-role-of-cartoonists-in-the-real-world

Jones, A., creator. (2017). Tuck Buckford takes on 'evil' Alex Jones. *Infowars*, June 22. Retrieved from https://www.infowars.com/tuck-buckford-takes-on-evil-alex-jones/

Jones, F. (2007). *Juvenal and the satiric genre*. London: Duckworth.

Jones, J. P. (2010). *Entertaining politics: Satiric television and political engagement* (2nd ed.). Lanham, MD: Rowan and Littlefield.

Jones, O. (2014). Laugh if you like. But we need satire more than ever. *The Guardian*, December 7. Retrieved from https://www.theguardian.com/commentisfree/2014/dec/07/laugh-satire-establishment-ridicule-democracy

Juntwait, K. (2017). 30 Times Samantha Bee destroyed Donald Trump. *Last Night On*, March. Retrieved from http://lastnighton.com/2017/02/27/30-times-samantha-bee-destroyed-donald-trump/

Juvenal. (2004). Satire I. In S. M. Braund (Ed. & Trans.), *Juvenal and Persius* (pp. 130–145). Cambridge, MA: Harvard University Press.

Kalle, M., & von Uslar, M. (2016). Ich Bin Gespannt, Wer Zuletzt Lacht. *Die Zeit*, May 12. Retrieved from http://www.zeit.de/2016/20/jan-boehmermann-interview-schmaehkritik

Katz, E., & Foulkes, D. (1962). On the use of the mass media as 'escape': Clarification of a concept. *Public Opinion Quarterly*, 26(3), 377–388.

Keane, C. (2015). *Juvenal and the satiric emotions*. Oxford: Oxford University Press.

Kercher, S. E. (2006). *Revel with a cause: Liberal satire in Postwar America*. Chicago, IL: University of Chicago Press.

Kernan, A. B. (1959). *The plot of satire*. New Haven, CT: Yale University Press.

Key, F. S. (1814). Defence of Fort M'Henry [aka lyrics to "The star-spangled banner"]. Self-published. Retrieved from https://www.loc.gov/item/ihas.100010457

Khan, I. A. (2018). Humour is the main measure of sanity. *Blog of the Bearded One*, November 18. Retrieved from https://blogofthebeardedone.wordpress.com/2018/11/18/humour-is-the-main-measure-of-sanity-2/

King Staff. (2012). *Candy Crush Saga*. King. Various platforms.

Kivistö, S. (2009). *Medical analogy in Latin satire*. Basingstoke: Palgrave.

Kleinman, A. (1988). *Illness narratives: Suffering, healing, and the human condition*. New York, NY: Basic Books.

Knechtges, D. R. (1971). Wit, humor, and satire in early Chinese literature (to A.D. 220). *Monumenta Serica: Journal of Oriental Studies, 29*, 79–98.

Korsemeyer, C. (2004). *Gender and aesthetics: An introduction*. New York, NY: London.

Kubrick, S. (1963). How I learned to stop worrying and love the cinema. *Films and Filming*, June, 12–13.

Kubrick, S., director. (1964). *Dr. Strangelove or: How I learned to stop worrying and love the bomb*. Los Angeles, CA: Columbia Pictures.

Kuiper, N. A. (2012). Humor and resiliency: Towards a process model of coping and growth. *Europe's Journal of Psychology, 8*(3), 475–491.

Kuiper, N. A., & Cann, A. (2014). Research on the role of humor in well-being and health. *Europe's Journal of Psychology, 10*(3), 412–428.

Kuiper, N. A., Grimshaw, M., Leite, C., & Kirsh, G. (2004). Humor is not always the best medicine: Specific components of sense of humor and psychological well-being. *Humor, 17*(1–2), 135–168.

Kuiper, N. A., & Martin, R. A. (2016). Three decades investigating humor and laughter: An interview with Professor Rod Martin. *Europe's Journal of Psychology, 12*(3), 498–512.

Kuiper, N. A., Martin, R. A., & Olinger, J. L. (1993). Coping humour, stress, and cognitive appraisals. *Canadian Journal of Behavioural Science, 25*(1), 81–96.

Kupfer, J. H. (1983). *Experience as art: Aesthetics in everyday life*. Albany, NY: State University of New York Press.

Larmer, B. (2011). Where an Internet joke is not just a joke. *The New York Times Magazine*, October 26. Retrieved from https://www.nytimes.com/2011/10/30/magazine/the-dangerous-politics-of-internet-humor-in-china.html

Lavelle, D. (2018). What happened next? The Trump Baby blimp: 'In retrospect, we should have ordered a bigger balloon'. *The Guardian*, December 17. Retrieved from https://www.theguardian.com/global/2018/dec/17/what-happened-next-the-trump-baby-blimp-in-retrospect-we-should-have-ordered-a-bigger-balloon

Lawton, G. (2019). If we label eco-anxiety as an illness, climate denialists have won. *New Scientist*, October 9. Retrieved from https://www.newscientist.com/article/mg24432512-900-if-we-label-eco-anxiety-as-an-illness-climate-denialists-have-won/#ixzz620mSmm6K

Lazarus, R. (1991). *Emotion and adaptation*. New York, NY: Oxford University Press.

Lee, S., creator. (2014). Satire. *Stewart Lee's comedy vehicle. BBC2*, March 15.

Lefcourt, H. M. (2001). *Humor: The psychology of living buoyantly*. New York, NY: Kluwer Academic.

Leonard, A. (2015). Capitalism must die! Your economic guidebook to revolution. *Rabble*, September 10. Retrieved from http://rabble.ca/books/reviews/2015/09/capitalism-must-die-your-economic-guidebook-to-revolution

Lindemann, H. (2001). *Damaged identities, narrative repair*. Ithaca, NY: Cornell University Press.

Lintott, S. (2016). Superiority in humor theory. *Journal of Aesthetics and Art Criticism*, *74*(4), 347–358.

Lintott, S. (2020). Stand-up comedy and mental health: Critiquing the mad stand-up stereotype. In P. A. Oppliger & E. Shouse (Eds.), *The dark side of stand-up comedy* (pp. 197–222). Basingstoke: Palgrave Macmillan.

Luckerson, V. (2015). How the 'John Oliver effect' is having a real-life impact. *Time*, July 10. Retrieved from https://time.com/3674807/john-oliver-net-neutrality-civil-forfeiture-miss-america/

MacDonald, H. (2013). Why Seth MacFarlane is not a great satirist. *The Beat*, February 27. Retrieved from http://www.comicsbeat.com/why-seth-macfarlane-is-not-a-great-satirist/

MacDowell, J. (2016). *Irony in film*. Houndmills: Palgrave Macmillan.

MacInnes, P. (2019). Future shock: Why *Years and Years* is 2019's most terrifying TV show. *The Guardian*, June 18. Retrieved from https://www.theguardian.com/tv-and-radio/2019/jun/18/years-and-years-2019-terrifying-tv-show-russell-t-davies

Magary, D. (2016). Watch John Oliver MURDERSLAY Donald Trump. *Deadspin*, February 29. Retrieved from https://theconcourse.deadspin.com/watch-john-oliver-murderslay-donald-trump-1761920331

Mann, M. E., & Toles, T. (2016). *The madhouse effect: How climate change denial is threatening our planet, destroying our politics, and driving us crazy.* New York, NY: Columbia University Press.

Marchese, D. (2016). In conversation: John Oliver. *Vulture*, February 22. Retrieved from http://www.vulture.com/2016/02/john-oliver-last-week-tonight-c-v-r.html

Marchese, D. (2019). Stephen Colbert on the political targets of satire. *The New York Times Magazine*, May 31. Retrieved from https://www.nytimes.com/interactive/2019/06/03/magazine/stephen-colbert-politics-religion.html

Martin, R. A. (2004). Sense of humor and physical health: Theoretical issues, recent findings, and future directions. *Humor: International Journal of Humor Research, 17*(1–2), 1–19.

Martin, R. A. (2006). *The psychology of humor. An integrative approach.* Burlington, MA: Elsevier.

Martin, R. A., Puhlik-Doris, P., Larsen, G., Gray, J., & Weir, K. (2003). Individual differences in uses of humor and their relation to psychological well-being: Development of the humor styles questionnaire. *Journal of Research in Personality, 37*(1), 48–75.

Matheson, C. (2001). *The Simpsons*, hyper-irony, and the meaning of life. In W. Irwin, M. Conard, & A. Skoble (Eds.), *The Simpsons and philosophy: The D'oh of Homer* (pp. 108–125). Chicago, IL: Open Court.

May, T. (2018). Prime Minister's speech on the environment. *GOV.UK*, January 11. Retrieved from https://www.gov.uk/government/ speeches/prime-ministers-speech-on-the-environment-11-january-2017

Maynard, P. (2012). What's so funny? Comic content in depiction. In A. Meskin & R. Cook (Eds.), *The art of comics: A philosophical approach* (pp. 105–124). Malden, MA: Wiley-Blackwell.

McClennen, S. (2011). *Colbert's America: Satire and democracy.* London: Palgrave MacMillan.

McClennen, S. (2016). 'The daily show' is dead to me: Trevor Noah will never, ever be good at his job—Also, thanks a lot for Donald Trump. *Salon*, May 16. Retrieved from http://www.salon.com/2016/05/16/the_daily_show_is_dead_to_me_trevor_noah_will_never_ever_be_good_at_his_job_also_thanks_a_lot_for_donald_trump

McClennen, S., & Maisel, R. (2014). *Is satire saving our nation? Mockery and American politics*. New York, NY: Palgrave McMillan.

McCreaddie, M., & Wiggins, S. (2008). The purpose and function of humour in health, health care and nursing: A narrative review. *Journal of Advanced Nursing*, *61*(6), 584–595.

McFarlane, S., host. (2013). *85th Academy Awards*. *ABC*, February 24.

McGruder, A. (2000). *The Boondocks. Because I know you don't read the newspaper*. Kansas City, MO: Andrews McMeel.

McGruder, A. (2001). *Fresh for '01… You Suckas!* Kansas City, MO: Andrews McMeel.

McMillan, S. (2015). *Capitalism must die! A basic introduction to capitalism: What it is, why it sucks, and how to crush it*. S.l.: Idées Nouvelles Idées Prolétariennes.

McQuail, D., Blumler, J. & Brown, J. (1972). The television audience: A revised perspective. In D. McQuail (Ed.), *Sociology of mass communication* (pp. 135–165). Middlesex: Penguin.

Meijer Drees, M., & Nieuwenhuis, I. B. (2010). De Macht van Satire: Grenzen Testen, Grenzen Stellen. *Nederlandse Letterkunde*, *15*(3), 193–220.

Morgan, R. (2019). The story behind the baby Trump balloon. *Fortune*, June 8. Retrieved from https://fortune.com/2019/06/08/baby-trump-balloon/

Mulkerrins, J. (2018). 'I've gone full witch': The fire and fury of TV satirist Samantha Bee. *The Guardian*, January 27. Retrieved from https://www.theguardian.com/culture/2018/jan/27/ive-gone-full-witch-the-fire-and-fury-of-tv-satirist-samantha-bee

Nachman, G. (2003). *Seriously funny: The rebel comedians of the 1950s and 1960s*. New York, NY: Pantheon Books.

Nagel, T. (1979/2012). *Mortal questions*. Cambridge: Cambridge University Press.

Nehring, A. (2013). Iran's Jon Stewart serves up illegal political satire. *The Atlantic*, June 11. Retrieved from https://www.theatlantic.com/international/archive/2013/06/irans-jon-stewart-serves-up-illegal-political-satire/276747/

Nevins, J. (2018). Three identical strangers: The bizarre tale of triplets separated at birth. *The Guardian*, June 28. Retrieved from https://www.theguardian.com/film/2018/jun/28/three-identical-strangers-the-bizarre-tale-of-triplets-separated-at-birth

Nguyen, C. T. (2019). Autonomy and aesthetic engagement. *Mind*. [Advance article]. Retrieved from https://doi.org/10.1093/mind/fzz054

NHS Staff. (2020). Mental wellbeing while staying at home. *NHS*. Retrieved from https://www.nhs.uk/oneyou/every-mind-matters/coronavirus-covid-19-staying-at-home-tips/

Nicholson, R. (2017). The Handmaid's tale review – Timely adaptation scares with dystopian dread. *The Guardian*, April 26. Retrieved from https://www.theguardian.com/tv-and-radio/2017/apr/26/the-handmaids-tale-tv-show-hulu-review

Nietzsche, F. (1882/2001). *The gay science. With a prelude in German rhymes* (B. Williams, Ed., Trans. J. Nauckhoff, and poems Trans. A. Del Caro). Cambridge: Cambridge University Press.

Njoya, W. (2017). Who's laughing now? Satire as a form of social protest. *The Elephant*, August 24. Retrieved from: https://www.theelephant.info/ideas/2017/08/24/whos-laughing-now-satire-as-a-form-of-social-protest/

Nokes, D. (1987). *Raillery and rage: A study of eighteenth century satire*. Hemel Hempstead: Harvester Press.

O'Hara, M. (2016). A serious business: What can comedy do? *Mosaic*, August 22. Retrieved from https://mosaicscience.com/story/comedy-humour-jokes-political-satire-taboo/

Oates, J. C. (2006, November 2). *Margaret Atwood's tale. The New York review of books*. Retrieved from http://www.nybooks.com/articles/2006/11/02/margaret-atwoods-tale/

Oliver, J., host. (2019). Gurbanguly Berdimuhamedov. *Last Week Tonight with John Oliver*. HBO, August 11. Retrieved from https://www.youtube.com/watch?v=-9QYu8LtH2E

Parker, R. (2016). 'Last Week Tonight' has sold more than 50,000 'Drumpf' Hats. *Hollywood Reporter*, June 23. Retrieved from https://www.hollywoodreporter.com/news/john-olivers-drumpf-hats-more-905892

Parker, T., & Stone, M., creators. (2006). Cartoon wars Part 1. *South Park*. Comedy Central, April 5.

Parker, T., & Stone, M., creators. (2013). The hobbit. *South Park*. Comedy Central, December 11.

Pascal, B. (1670/1910). *Thoughts* (Trans. W. F. Trotter). London: P.F. Collier & Son.

Paul, K. (2020). It's Corona time: TikTok helps teens cope with the Coronavirus pandemic. *The Guardian*, March 12. Retrieved from https://www.theguardian.com/world/2020/mar/12/coronavirus-outbreak-tik-tok-memes

Pennacchia, R. (2017). Let's hope Alex Jones attacking a Trump Piñata is the weirdest thing you see all day. *Someecards*, June 26. Retrieved from https://www.someecards.com/news/politics/alex-jones-trump-pinata-video/

Perkins, D. [Tom Tomorrow, pseud.]. (1993). This modern world. *Peace Review*, *5*(2), 209–215.

Perkins, D. [Tom Tomorrow, pseud.]. (2013). Transcript of winner's speech. *Herblock Foundation*. Retrieved from http://www.herbblockfoundation.org/herblock-prize/prize-winners/dan-perkins-aka-tom-tomorrow

Perkins, D. [Tom Tomorrow, pseud.]. (2014a). The very naughty whistleblower. *Sparky's List*, July 13. Mailing list.

Perkins, D. [Tom Tomorrow, pseud.]. (2014b). Approved responses. *Sparky's List*, August 24. Mailing list.

Perkins, D. [Tom Tomorrow, pseud.]. (2016). *25 Years of tomorrow* (Vols. 1 and 2). Tomorowco Industries.

Perkins, D. [Tom Tomorrow, pseud.]. (n.d.). Endorsement by Ben Bagdikian. *This Modern World*. Retrieved from http://thismodernworld.com/about

Peterson, R. (2008). *Strange bedfellows: How late-night comedy turns democracy into a joke*. New Brunswick, NJ: Rutgers University Press.

Pierquet, B. (2018). Political burnout: When politics make you (poli) sick. *Medium*, December 6. https://medium.com/@brie_25021/political-burnout-when-politics-make-you-poli-sick-aaff6cc1b8c3

Plante, C. N., Gentile, D. A., Groves, C. L., Modlin, A., & Blanco-Herrera, J. (2019). Video games as coping mechanisms in the etiology of video game addiction. *Psychology of Popular Media Culture*, *8*(4), 385–394.

Plato. (1973). *Phaedrus and the seventh and eighth letters* (Ed. & Trans. W. Hamilton). Harmondsworth: Penguin.

Pollard, A. (1970). *Satire*. London: Methuen.

Poniewozik, J. (2019). Review: In 'Years and Years,' things fall apart, fast. *The New York Times*, June 23. Retrieved from https://www.nytimes.com/2019/06/23/arts/television/years-and-years-review-hbo.html

Poole, J. (1657). *The English Parnassus, or, a Helpe to English Poesie*. London: Tho. Johnson. Retrieved from https://search.proquest.com/eebo/docview/2248498761/8199759/1D4DE64B755F4A35PQ/1?accountid=7408.

Procassini, I. (2017). Samantha Bee: Comedy, politics, and catharsis. *Northwestern Business Review*, March 2. Retrieved from https://northwesternbusinessreview.org/samantha-bee-comedy-politics-and-catharsis-58f8f13cef77

Quirk, S. (2015). *Why stand-up matters. How comedians manipulate and influence*. London: Bloomsbury Methuen.

Rabin, N. (2005). Aaron McGruder. *The A.V. Club*, November 23. Retrieved from http://www.avclub.com/article/aaron-mcgruder-13965

Radloff, J. (2014). Seth MacFarlane wants to talk: The *Family Guy* creator on his holiday album and his softer side. *Glamour*, November 12. Retrieved from https://www.glamour.com/story/seth-macfarlane-wants-to-talk

Rall, T. (Ed.). (2002). *Attitude. The new subversive political cartoonists*. New York, NY: NBM Publishing.

Randolph, M. C. (1941). The medical concept in English renaissance satiric theory: Its possible relationships and implications. *Studies in Philology*, *38*(2), 125–157.

Reed, R. (2016). Watch John Oliver annihilate Donald Trump, re-brand 'Drumpf'. *Rolling Stone*, February 29. Retrieved from http://www.rollingstone.com/tv/news/watch-john-oliver-annihilate-donald-trump-re-brand-drumpf-20160229

RFE/RL Staff. (2009). Jon Stewart on political satire in a free and democratic society. *RadioFreeEurope RadioLiberty*, May 11. https://www.rferl.org/a/Jon_Stewart_On_Political_Satire_In_A_Free_Society/1683301.html

Riddle, K., Peebles, A., Davis, C., Xu, F., & Schroeder, E. (2018). The addictive potential of television binge watching: Comparing intentional and unintentional binges. *Psychology of Popular Media Culture*, 7(4), 589–604.

Rnic, K., Dozois, D. J. A., & Martin, R. A. (2016). Cognitive distortions, humor styles, and depression. *Europe's Journal of Psychology*, *12*(3), 348–362.

Roach, J., director. (1997). *Austin Powers: International man of mystery*. Burbank, CA: New Line Cinema.

Roberts, D. (Ed.). (2001). *Gulliver's travels, by Jonathan Swift*. Ware: Wordsworth Editions.

Roberts, G. (1999). Introduction: A story of stories. In G. Roberts & J. Holmes (Eds.), *Healing stories: Narrative in psychiatry and psychotherapy* (pp. 3–26). Oxford: Oxford University Press.

Robinson, F. N. (1912/2017). J. W. Hurley (Ed.). *Druids, bards, satirists and enchanters: In early Irish literature.* Scotts Valley: CreateSpace.

Robinson, J. (2004). *Deeper than reason: Emotion and its role in literature, music, and art.* Oxford: Oxford University Press.

Robinson, J. (2020). Aesthetic emotions. *The Monist, 103*(2), 205–222.

Robinson, M. J., & Knobloch-Westerwick, S. (2016). Mood management through selective media use for health and well-being. In L. Reinecke & M. B. Oliver (Eds.), *The Routledge handbook of media use and well-being* (pp. 65–79). New York, NY: Routledge.

Roiland, J., & Dan, H., creators. (2020). Never Ricking Morty. *Rick and Morty*. Adult Swim, May 3.

Ronson, J. (2011). *The psychopath test.* London: Picador.

Roos, J., guest. (2017). Pauw en Jinek. *NPO1*, February 28. Retrieved from https://www.youtube.com/watch?v=XzvEK_l6Hlk

Rothstein, M. (1986). No balm in Gilead for Margaret Atwood. *The New York Times*, February 17. Retrieved from http://www.nytimes.com/books/00/09/03/specials/atwood-gilead.html

RT Staff. (2019). Years and Years: Series 1 (2019). *Rotten Tomatoes.* Retrieved from https://www.rottentomatoes.com/tv/years_and_years/s01

Schur, M., creator. (2017). Everything is great! *The Good Place. NBC*, September 20.

Schur, M., creator. (2019a). Chidi sees the time-knife. *The Good Place. NBC*, January 17.

Schur, M., creator. (2019b). The book of Dougs. *The Good Place. NBC*, January 10.

Seven Stories Staff. (2013). The minimum security chronicles. Resistance to ecocide. *Seven Stories Press.* Retrieved from https://www.sevenstories.com/books/3700-the-minimum-security-chronicles

Shedler, J. (2014). Genius and depression from the same well? *Psychology Today*, August 15. Retrieved from https://www.psychologytoday.com/gb/blog/psychologically-minded/201408/genius-and-depression-the-same-well

Sherry, J. L. (2004). Flow and media enjoyment. *Communication Theory, 14*(4), 328–347.

Shusterman, R. (2003). Entertainment: A question for aesthetics. *British Journal of Aesthetics, 43*(3), 289–307.

Shusterman, R. (2008). Aesthetic experience. From analysis to *Eros*. In R. Shusterman & A. Tomlin (Eds.), *Aesthetic experience* (pp. 79–97). London: Routledge.

Silvia, P. J. (2005). What is interesting? Exploring the appraisal structure of interest. *Emotion, 5*(1), 89–102.

Sliter, M., Kale, A., & Yuan, Z. (2014). Is humor the best medicine? The buffering effect of coping humor on traumatic stressors in firefighters. *Journal of Organizational Behavior, 35*(2), 257–272.

Sloterdijk, P. (1987). *Critique of cynical reason* (Trans. M. Eldred). Minneapolis, MN: University of Minnesota Press.

Smug Staff. (2019). About Smug. *Smug*. Retrieved from http://smugwinchester.com/about-2/

Solomon, D. (2005). Funny about the news. *New York Times*, September 25. Retrieved from https://www.nytimes.com/2005/09/25/magazine/funny-about-the-news.html

Sorensen, J. (2008). *Slowpoke. One nation, oh my god!* Brooklyn, NY: Ig Publishing.

Sorensen, J. (2014). *Transcript of winner's speech. Herblock Foundation.* Retrieved from http://www.herbblockfoundation.org/herblock-prize/prize-winners/jen-sorensen

Sperber, D., & Wilson, D. (2012). *Meaning and relevance.* Cambridge, MA: Cambridge University Press.

Spiegel Staff. (2016). Erdogan and the satirist. Inside Merkel's comedy conundrum. *Spiegel Online*, April 15. Retrieved from http://www.spiegel.de/international/germany/germany-green-lights-legal-case-against-erdogan-critical-comic-a-1087445-3.html

Stam, R. (1989). *Subversive pleasures: Bakhtin, cultural criticism, and film.* Baltimore, MD: Johns Hopkins University Press.

Stecker, R. (2010). *Aesthetics and the philosophy of art* (2nd ed.). Lanham, MD: Rowman & Littlefield.

Stoeber, J., Harris, R. A., & Moon, P. S. (2007). Perfectionism and the experience of pride, shame, and guilt: Comparing healthy perfectionists, unhealthy perfectionists, and non-perfectionists. *Personality and Individual Differences*, *43*, 131–141.

Stoknes, P. E. (2015). *What we think about when we try not to think about global warming*. Vermont, VT: Chelsea Green.

Stratyner, L., & Keller, J. R.. (2009). Introduction: An unofficial explanation and brief history of *South Park*. In L. Stratyner & J. R. Keller (Eds.), *The deep end of South Park: Critical essays on television's shocking cartoon series* (pp. 1–14). Jefferson, NC: McFarland & Company.

Sugerman, J. (2016). They're not eviscerating Trump: John Oliver and Stephen Colbert will never save us from fascism. *Salon*, March 12. Retrieved from http://www.salon.com/2016/03/12/none_of_them_are_beating_trump_john_oliver_and_stephen_colbert_will_never_save_us_from_fascism

Suits, B. (2014). *The grasshopper* (3rd ed.). Peterborough: Broadview Press.

Sutherland, J. (1958). *English satire*. Cambridge, MA: Cambridge University Press.

SW Staff. (2019). 21 Minutes of the most devastating insults: Watch John Oliver absolutely destroy Donald Trump. *Scoop Whoop*, May 1. Retrieved from https://www.scoopwhoop.com/21-Minutes-Of-The-Most-Devastating-Insults-Watch-John-Oliver-Absolutely-Destroy-Donald-Trump/

Swanigan, P. (2012). Much the same on the other side: *The Boondocks* and the symbolic frontier. *Children's Literature*, *40*, 28–48.

Swift, J. (1704/2009). *A tale of a tub*. Auckland: Floating Press.

Swift, J. (1729). A modest proposal. Retrieved from https://en.wikisource.org/wiki/A_Modest_Proposal

Steele, P. (1978). *Jonathan Swift. Preacher and Jester*. Oxford: Clarendon Press.

Szabo, A. (2011). The acute effects of humor and exercise on mood and anxiety. *Journal of Leisure Research*, *35*(2), 152–162.

Taylor, C. (2004). Jon Stewart: Crossfire 'hurting America.' *Salon*, October 16. Retrieved from https://www.salon.com/2004/10/15/crossfire_2/

Televisió de Catalunya Staff. (2009). *Gladiators*. Retrieved from https://www.youtube.com/watch?v=TlVnj22axmU

Test, G. A. (1991). *Satire: Spirit and art*. Gainesville, FL: University Press of Florida.

Thompson, S. (2000). Tom Lehrer. *The A.V. Club*, May 24. Retrieved from http://www.avclub.com/article/tom-lehrer-13660

Tiberius, V. (2008). *The reflective life: Living wisely with our limits*. Oxford: Oxford University Press.

TMZ Staff. (2014). Comedian John Oliver's bringing down of the FCC's website makes him a powerful Americans [*sic.*]! *TMZ*, June 6. Retrieved from https://www.youtube.com/watch?v=cMwJkyzXv8k

Trumpbabyuk. (2019). Bring Trump Baby back. *Crowdfunder*. Retrieved from https://www.crowdfunder.co.uk/bring-the-baby-back

Tucholsky, K. (1919). Was darf die Satire? *Berliner Tageblatt*. 36. Retrieved from https://de.wikisource.org/wiki/Was_darf_die_Satire%3F_(Tucholsky)

Tucker, R. P., Judah, M. R., O'Keefe, V. M., Mills, A. C., Lechner, W. V., Davidson, C. L., … Wingate, L. R. (2013). Humor styles impact the relationship between symptoms of social anxiety and depression. *Personality and Individual Differences*, *55*(7), 823–827.

Turner, P. (Ed.). (1985). Jonathan Swift. *Gulliver's travels*. Oxford: Oxford University Press.

Vankadara, H. (2017). Why news is best served with satire. *LinkedIn*, April 14. Retrieved from https://www.linkedin.com/pulse/why-news-best-served-satire-harika-vankadara

Veatch, T. C. (1998). A theory of humor. *Humor: International Journal of Humor Research*, *11*(2), 161–215.

Vickerstaff, A. (2019). We're flying the Trump baby blimp again – Because the US President doesn't deserve our respect. *The Independent*, June 3. Retrieved from https://www.independent.co.uk/voices/trump-uk-visit-baby-blimp-protests-london-parliament-square-a8941446.html

Wallace, J. M. (2001). A (Karl, not Groucho) Marxist in Springfield. In W. Irwin, M. Conard, & A. Skoble (Eds.), *The Simpsons and philosophy: The D'oh of Homer* (pp. 235–251). Chicago, IL: Open Court.

Weaver, S. (2018). Suffering from Brexit anxiety? You could get free counselling. *The Guardian*, June 9. Retrieved from https://www.theguardian.com/politics/2018/jun/09/suffering-from-brexit-anxiety-you-could-get-free-counselling

Webber, J. (2013). *The cultural set up of comedy: Affective politics in the United States Post 9/11*. Bristol: Intellect.

Wellek, R., & Warren, A. (1966). *Theory of literature* (3rd ed.). London: Cape.

Welsch, W. (2005). Sport viewed aesthetically, and even as art? In A. Light & J. M. Smith (Eds.), *The aesthetics of everyday life* (pp. 135–155). New York, NY: Columbia University Press.

Wheeler, B. (2017). Full frontal with Samantha Bee's Allana Harkin on the catharsis of making fun of Trump. *The Globe and Mail*, April 26. Retrieved from https://www.theglobeandmail.com/arts/television/full-frontal-with-samantha-bees-allana-harkin-on-the-catharsis-of-making-fun-of-trump/article34823493/

Wight, J. D. (1936/1964). *Roman satire: Its outlook on social life*. Hampton: Archon.

Williams, B. (2001). Introduction. In Friedrich Nietzsche. (1882). *The Gay Science. With a Prelude in German Rhymes*, edited by Bernard Williams, translated by Josefine Nauckhoff, and poems translated by Adrian Del Caro (pp. vii–xxiii). Cambridge, MA: Cambridge University Press.

Williams, B. (2002). *Truth and truthfulness*. Princeton, NJ: Princeton University Press.

Wilson, C.-J. (2002). Crossdresser and cartoonist. *Transgender Tapestry*, 97, 24–25.

Witke, C. (1970). *Latin satire: The structure of persuasion*. Leiden: Brill.

Wittenberg, H. (2014). The Boer and the Jackal: Satire and resistance in Khoi Orature. *Critical Arts*, *28.4*, 593–609.

Woods, A. (2011). The limits of narrative: Provocations for the medical humanities. *Medical Humanities*, *37*(2), 73–78.

Young, D. G. (2018). Theories and effects of political humor: discounting cues, gateways, the impact of incongruities. In K. Kenski & K. H. Jamieson (Eds.), *The Oxford Handbook of Political Communication* (pp. 872–884). Oxford: Oxford University Press.

Young, D. G. R., Holbert, L., & Jamieson, K. H. (2014). Successful practices for the strategic use of political parody and satire. *American Behavioral Scientist*, *58*(9), 1111–1130.

Youssef, B. (2017). *Revolution for dummies*. New York, NY: HarperCollins.

Younge, G. (2005). Strip tease. *The Guardian*, December 22. Retrieved from https://www.theguardian.com/artanddesign/2005/dec/22/art.usa

Zakari, J. (2013). Oscar producers Meron and Zadan defend Seth MacFarlane, boob song: Complainers 'missed the joke'. *The Hollywood*

Reporter, March 16. Retrieved from https://www.hollywoodreporter.com/news/oscar-producers-meron-zadan-defend-429265

Zautra, A. J., Sheets, V. L., & Sandler, I. N. (1996). An examination of the construct validity of coping dispositions for a sample of recently divorced mothers. *Psychological Assessment*, *8*(3), 256–264.

Zeit Staff. (2016). Schmähgedicht über Erdoğan wird in Teilen Verboten. *Die Zeit*, May 17. Retrieved from http://www.zeit.de/kultur/2016-05/landgericht-hamburg-verbietet-passagen-von-boehmermanns-schmaehgedicht

Žižek, S. (1989). *The sublime object of ideology*. London: Verso.

INDEX

Note: Page numbers followed by "*n*" indicate notes.

Printed and bound by CPI Group (UK) Ltd, Croydon, CR0 4YY
16/09/2026
14963171-0001